HOW TO START A 6-FIGURE PROPERTY SOURCING BUSINESS

Property Sourcing Secrets

KATIE ORR

Copyright © 2022
Katie Orr
How to Start a 6-Figure Property Sourcing Business
Property Sourcing Secrets
All rights reserved.

No part of this publication may be reproduced, distributed, or transmitted in any form or by any means, including photocopying, recording, or other electronic or mechanical methods, without the prior written permission of the publisher, except in the case of brief quotations embodied in critical reviews and certain other non-commercial uses permitted by copyright law.

Katie Orr

Printed in the United States of America
First Printing 2022
First Edition 2022

10 9 8 7 6 5 4 3 2 1

How to Start a 6-Figure Property Sourcing Business

Table of Contents

Introduction 1
    Disclaimer 12
What Is Property Sourcing 13
    What Is a Property Sourcer? 13
    What Does a Property Sourcer Do? 14
    Why Do People Work with Property Sourcers? 15
How to Find Deals 17
    Where to Find Deals 19
    Go and Do It 33
How to Approach Deals 34
    Deal Review 34
    Viewings 35
    Builder Quotes 37
    Negotiation 38
    Go and Do It 42
How to Find Investors 44
    Social Media 44
    How to Have the Most Impact on Social Media 49
    Email List 59
    Publications and Media 63
    Paid Ads 65
    Client Acquisition Tools 65
    Go and Do It 71
Building a Relationship with Investors 73
    Client Journey 73
    Nurturing Clients via Email or Social Channels - KNOW LIKE TRUST 74
    Phone call 78
    Go and Do It 83

The Sales Process 85
    How We Created Our Sales Process 85
    Know the Product 89
    Present the Deal 90
    Chat With Qualified Buyers 92
    Reservation 95
    Memorandum of Sale 99
    How to Structure Your Fees 100
    Create Raving Fans Who Come Back for More 102
    Go and Do It 110

Progression 112
    Communication 114
    Consistency 115
    Clarity 116
    Go and Do It 117

Starting Your Property Sourcing Business 118
    Compliance 118
    £500 Property Sourcing Business 122
    Go and Do It 123

Scaling Your Property Sourcing Business 125
    Other Ways to Maximise Income 135
    Go and Do It 139

Mindset 141
    Time 143
    Set Goals 144
    Believe In the Service You Provide 147
    Go and Do It 148

Replicate Success 149

Introduction

Everything changed for me on the 26th of December 2020 (Boxing Day).

Before that day, like most, I followed the regular path. I finished school and took a corporate job. I didn't go to university because I wasn't sure what I wanted to do, so instead, I started an apprenticeship within an insurance company's IT department. When I say I joined fresh out of school, I mean I was FRESH out of school. Being very green to the professional world, my first few months were a crash course in learning how to navigate a professional environment. I learned how to answer phones, what was expected of me in a professional environment, the ins and outs of email etiquette, and how to work to deadlines. The environment I worked in was very empowering. My team were big on constantly looking for ways to automate or streamline processes to increase output. If I went back and did it all again, I wouldn't change a thing. The skills I learned there were a fantastic foundation for when I started my business.

At that time, my goal was to buy my own place. I wanted a place to call my own, and I thought, wow, if I had a house, that would be me set. Unfortunately, for my big aspirations, my starting salary was only £12,000 per year. Even if I found a way to spend next to nothing, it would take me 100 years to save enough to buy a house. Not quite the timeline I had in mind!

So, I did what any Gen Z would do and turned to Google for answers. I started consuming all the information I could get my hands on. I became addicted to self-development and read everything I could find on how to develop my finances, health, and business. My parents were blown away by this because I have dyslexia, and it was a struggle to get me to read anything growing up. I used to hate reading with a passion, but it must have been the reading material because I was inhaling these business books. I would finish a business book in a weekend because I was so engaged with what I was reading.

These books made me even more passionate about my goal of owning my own home. I spent every spare moment learning everything I could about what I needed to do to achieve it. It became my passion, my obsession. I worked hard, saved a lot, and looked at the property market every day. As I built my knowledge, I started writing about what I was learning on my blog. At the start, I had very few readers. I don't even think my parents were reading my blog. Each week I would share a property I liked or thought was a good deal on my blog.

THE ORIGINAL BLOG:

And that brings us to Boxing Day 2020. The UK was in the middle of a seemingly endless lockdown. Everything was closed, and daily walks were the only break we had from being cooped up in our homes. My family and I went for a walk to do a little bit of property window shopping. We couldn't visit the properties for inspections because of the lockdown, but we created a bit of a walking tour and saw the outside of the properties.

I found a property that I thought was a fantastic flip project and wanted to share it on my blog and social media. So, I asked my younger brother to take a video of me pointing and dancing in front of the property. It took a lot of convincing my brother because he had no idea what I was doing and was cringing hard. He hurried me along because, apparently, it was embarrassing. Once I got back home, I added text over it to show the numbers behind the project and posted it. It was only a 10-second video, but it got a crazy response, 17,000 videos in the first 2 hours and 100,000 in the first 24 hours. The dance is now affectionately called "the wiggle" by my followers, and I have become known for doing "the wiggle" outside new properties.

My DMs were blowing up with people asking for my advice or asking me to find them a similar deal. The entrepreneur inside me, the one who had been binge-reading business books for years, lit up. I had found a way to monetise my blog. I started speaking to clients to understand what they were looking for. Armed with that knowledge, I went out and found properties that matched their needs. I had been doing it for a while before I found out the name for what I'd been doing, property sourcing. And I discovered it was a well-developed, thriving industry. I haven't looked back since.

My life looks very different now that I run my own business. While I was still working full-time, I achieved more than I could ever dream of in my first 12 months in business:

- I sold 90+ properties
- I earned over £100k
- I was featured in major publications like Business Insider and Vice
- I won industry awards
- I bought my own investment property with the profits from my business

I went from not knowing what property sourcing is to growing my business to out-earn my 9-5 – all without any previous experience in the property industry, just a passion for property and business. I built something of my own and was able to leave my job, which I will talk more about later. If you take one thing from my story, it's that you don't need years of experience to become a property sourcer.

Property sourcing has not only worked for me. Thousands of people have built businesses with unlimited earning potential and reclaimed their freedom. I believe there are 3 true freedoms in life:

1. Time Freedom – the ability to spend your time doing anything you like
2. Financial freedom – the freedom to never have to worry about money
3. Location freedom – the freedom to live and work anywhere in the world

My business gave me all 3 of those. I am writing this book in Dubai. I have been out here for a month, but I could live wherever I want in the world and still run my business. Starting a business is not something that you need a lot of money to do. I started my business from my bedroom, and I think I spent £500 in total the entire first year.

It has never been easier to start a business and take control of your life than it is now. The internet allows you to expand your reach, share ideas, and create the life you have always dreamed of. Financial freedom is now possible for everyone - regardless of their background and circumstances. Yes, some people have a head start; there is no denying that, but there is a wealth of resources available online. As long as you have access to the internet, there's an abundance of knowledge at your fingertips. You no longer have to go to a good school or have parents that know the right people to get ahead. The internet has levelled the playing field.

Our generation is the most entrepreneurial in history. Teenagers are out-earning their teachers before they leave school. They are making their fortunes on social media or leveraging skills learned on YouTube to start a business. No wonder children leaving school want to be TikTok stars and YouTubers. Their favourite influencers are relatable, ordinary people building a life of flexibility and freedom. That sounds a lot better than working a 9-5.

We are so lucky to be born in a time of technological advancements. 20 years ago, it wouldn't have been possible to start many of the businesses that exist today - and it definitely wouldn't have been possible to start a business the way I did. There were no social media platforms, and mobile devices couldn't access the internet.

Two decades ago, starting a business was a much larger undertaking. To be successful, you needed a high street presence and multiple staff members. There was no free marketing; you had to pay for TV ads, billboards, or ads in newspapers and magazines. All of this is extremely expensive, and your pool of customers was limited to your geographic area.

I am grateful that I was able to create the life of my dreams with minimal upfront cost. I started my property sourcing business, KO Estates, with just my phone and an internet connection. I spend every day helping people and doing what I love. Now, I want to help you to do the same.

Starting a business is not all sunshine and rainbows, though. 3 months in, I was ready to pack it all in. I was still working my 9-5 and doing deal sourcing part-time on top of all that, and I had not had a single sale. I couldn't understand it. After my first video, I had countless people telling me that they wanted this service. Where were they now? I was finding deals for several different types of properties, but I just couldn't get a deal over the line. I couldn't sell the very thing people were asking me for. At this point, I felt like I couldn't sell food to a starving crowd, and because of my 9-5, I was working around the clock and yet I had nothing to show for it.

I couldn't do it. I was tired and fed up. I wanted to give up. I was annoyed and frustrated that I had put my time into something and couldn't make it a success. Maybe having a business wasn't for me.

It was around that time, my Dad was looking to sell his investment property. He went to a local agent who told him to evict the tenant before he sold the property. The agent said that he would struggle to sell the property otherwise. The only thing is, Dad felt loyal to the tenant. They had lived in the property for years, had always looked after the property, and never missed a rent payment. After meeting with the agent, he spoke to me about it. I ran the numbers and saw that it would make an excellent investment for anyone. So, I offered to send it to my list. I had written off deal sourcing, but I said as a favour I could pop it out to my database.

I sat down at my laptop and wrote a message that I sent to my entire email list. I shared the details of the deal, attached some photos, and sent the email. I was still at my desk, catching up on emails, when I heard a ding. Someone had replied to my email 5 minutes after I had sent it. I was used to hearing nothing, so it was a shock. It was also a relief to know that I wasn't just emailing a ton of spam accounts.

It didn't stop there. A couple of minutes later, another investor emailed, and then another. By the end of the week, I had my first sale. I cried when the fee hit my account. My account had never received a payment like that before. What a moment!

My perspective changed at that moment. Suddenly it was possible. It would work. I could do it.

The analytical side of me needed to understand why I sold the deal. What was different? Was it just luck, or was there something about this deal that had people lining up to buy? There was only one way to find out. I spoke to the client. I asked them what stood out about this deal.

He told me that it was exactly what they needed. Everything was done for him. There was a tenant in place, and the property was ready to go. It was a walk-in investment opportunity where he could start making money right away. That was my lightbulb moment. It wasn't the properties that weren't working; it was how I packaged and sold them. People wanted convenience. It turns out a lot of my clients were not located nearby, so they needed everything in place to buy remotely. They needed me to do more than just find the deal; they needed me to be their eyes on the ground.

So, I did what all of the business books I read told me to do next. Once I found what worked, I did more of it.

Over the next 6 months, I refined the process. I learned something with every sale so I could continue to improve. I recorded and analysed every detail in my prospecting, networking, deal types, returns, and selling tactics. By bettering the process with every deal, I created a better experience for my clients. The end-to-end process was quicker and smoother. I was able to speed up my success. And that was how I was able to scale to 100 property sales in the first year. That's more than some estate agents.

I created a step-by-step strategy so I could replicate this success again and again. This strategy had 3 parts:

1. Finding Deals – Deals are like your inventory. If you have good deals, your clients will keep coming back.
2. Finding Investors – These are your clients. You need to know their wants and needs inside and out.
3. Making the Sale – Match the investor with the right deal and then create an irresistible offer that nobody could turn down. Make sure your deal makes it to completion because that's when you get paid.

This framework was a recipe for

- Finding the best deals in any market so I could build a pipeline off-market opportunities and make sure I always had an incredible supply
- Creating an unlimited number of leads so I had a list of investors hungry for my deals and could sell a property minutes after launching
- Scaling my business because I knew exactly what worked and doubled down until I secured 100 properties in the first year

This framework worked for me and my business. It's the framework I still use today. Last summer, I realised just how powerful it was.

My younger brother Tom, who was 17 at the time, was on summer holidays from school. He was telling me that he was looking for his first job because he was desperate to make some money to pay for a festival all his friends were going to. He knew a bit about what I was doing because he was often the cameraman for my videos. So, I said while you are looking, why don't you give sourcing a go? You have spare time, and if nothing else, you will learn from it. He accepted the challenge. I talked him through my framework and then left him to it. Based on his previous business experience, I didn't think much of it, to be honest.

His previous business idea went bankrupt a couple of weeks in. He sold hats on Depop via drop shipping. The issue was his hats took 21 days to come from China, and his customers paid for next-day delivery. You can imagine what happened, everyone reported the account, his PayPal got suspended, and he had to refund all the clients. On top of that, Tom couldn't cancel the orders, so his clients got a free refund and a free hat once it finally arrived. He was out of pocket for the cost of the hat, so his venture resulted in a loss. It's something we still laugh about now.

If I'm honest, I was not expecting much, but to my surprise, he called me within a few days to tell me he had sourced his first deal, and a week later, he had sold it. I almost dropped the phone! He was 17, still at school, and had sourced and sold a property. A deal with a £2,000 sourcing fee attached, which is a big payday for a 17-year-old. Forget drop shipping! My brother did that on his own, with no prior experience, just using the framework. I was ecstatic! That's when I realised how powerful this framework was. It could be applied by anyone and get results from a standing start. I was excited. I knew I had to share it with others so they could have the same opportunity.

I turned my framework into a programme, Property Sourcing Secrets, designed to take anyone from £0 to a six-figure sourcing business. I still use this framework today, and I'm going to share it with you in this book.

I like to joke that I fell into property sourcing, and I did - but my success was no accident, and it was definitely not overnight. I spent thousands of hours researching, learning, and building my business. It took a lot of work and a lot of trial and error to find my recipe for success.

While I was finding my feet, I experienced some incredible highs and devastating lows. Once I found what worked and repeated it, my business stabilised. Creating processes that can be replicated and scaled led to the speedy growth of KO Estates. Now, I teach others how to start and scale their property sourcing businesses. This book is a condensed version of everything I have learned in the process of starting and scaling my own business.

This book contains all the information I wish I had known when I started. I have written down all the lessons I learned the hard way so you can speed up your success. Learning from my mistakes will save you time, money, and headaches.

Each chapter will take you through the steps of becoming a property sourcer. I have simplified the process into 4 stages:

- How to find deals
- How to find investors

- How to secure the sale
- How to scale your business

The process is easy; the difficult part is executing each step. At the end of each chapter, there are actionable steps to take to put the knowledge to work. They are designed to help you implement the lessons as you go. I want you to be further ahead by the time you finish reading this book.

I wrote this book because property sourcing changed my life, and I know it can change yours too.

Disclaimer

I will never pretend to know everything. Even though I have achieved more than I could ever have imagined, I still have a lot to learn about business and property sourcing. This book was written to share my experiences and help others avoid the mistakes I made when I was just starting out.

I would encourage everyone to apply critical thinking to everything they read and learn. Consider if it is right for their business rather than just applying it blindly. Peeking behind the curtain of other businesses to see what you can learn will always be useful but pick and choose what you want to implement in your own business.

With that out of the way, let's get started!

What Is Property Sourcing

I had never heard of property sourcing before I started doing it; I was just someone who liked looking at real estate in their spare time. Imagine my surprise when I learned that it was a valid career option!

What Is a Property Sourcer?

If you already know what a property sourcer is and what they do, then feel free to skip over this part. I didn't know what a property sourcer was when I started my journey; it was something I fell into by accident. So, if you're starting where I did, then read on.

A property sourcer is someone who puts together property deals to sell to property investors. People tend to wonder how property sourcers are different to estate agents.

So, what's the difference between a property sourcer and an estate agent?

An estate agent works in an office as a part of a team. They represent the seller and operate in their best interests. Buyers come to an estate agent to see the properties they have on their books.

A property sourcer can work as part of a team, but often they work independently. They represent the buyer and proactively search for properties for their clients. They may even broker deals with the seller before presenting them to their clients. So, in the simplest terms, an estate agent works with the seller, and a property sourcer works for the buyer.

The property market in the UK is enormous. There are so many properties for sale, and some are better deals than others. Buyers don't always have time to scour property listings and definitely don't have time to view properties that show potential.

I like to think of what I do a little bit like matchmaking. When I view properties, I think about what type of buyer they would suit. Property investors come in all different forms and have a range of different needs. I match property investors with properties that tick all the boxes.

What Does a Property Sourcer Do?

A property sourcer finds a property that suits the requirements of a buyer. In my case, my buyers are looking for buy-to-let properties. I work to find them the best deal possible.

I don't just spend my time on Zoopla or Rightmove as many people may think. I use my network to secure off-market properties to present to my clients. While we represent the buyer first and foremost, the long-term success of our business relies on us creating mutually beneficial deals. Many of the deals I source come through referrals from past sellers who have worked with me and my team.

I broker the deal and then step back and let the buyer and seller's solicitors finalise the paperwork.

Why Do People Work with Property Sourcers?

The two things I hear most when I talk about property sourcing are:

- *"If the deal is so good, why don't you buy it yourself?"*
- *"Why would people work with a property sourcer when they can find a place themselves?"*

The answer to the first is that there are thousands of deals out there, and I don't have the resources to buy them all myself. (Not yet, anyway!)

Also, not every deal will be suitable for my needs, but that doesn't make them any less of a good deal. I love finding excellent deals, so instead of only looking for property deals when I have money to buy new properties, I source deals all year long for clients.

The second thing is something that every service-based business owner hears. Yes, some people would never work with a property sourcer because they don't like the thought of paying someone to do something they could do themselves. There will also be people who repair their sinks instead of hiring a plumber or do their taxes rather than hiring an accountant. This doesn't mean that everyone is willing to do those things themselves. There are lots of people out there who are happy to pay for services because they value the expertise of the person they work with, and it saves them a lot of time and effort.

The people I represent work with me because of one of the following things:

- Lack of time
- Need for expertise
- Both

I have the connections and know-how to find the best deals for my clients. The money they are saving on the deals more than covers my fees before we get into all the additional value I add.

Often, the buyers I work with are new to property investing and don't want to have to learn all about what makes a good investment property. They just want to buy a property and start making money. Know what your clients are looking for. Mine don't have the resources to find their ideal investment property as quickly as I can. More time equals more opportunities to make money for these types of investors. Let's jump in and see how we can actually make this happen.

How to Find Deals

What comes first, the deal or the investor? It's like the property sourcing version of the chicken or the egg. Personally, I like to find the deal first. If you find a good deal, then you can use it to attract investors. If you find the investor first, then you will be cornered into their criteria and dependent on their decision. Not to mention, it could take you a while to find the right deal and, therefore, make the sale. So, for me, the deals come first.

If you want your property sourcing business to be successful in the long term, you need good deals. When you have good deals, clients come back for more and tell their friends about you. That is how you win in the property sourcing game.

Your deals are your product. When you have a good product, and you go viral, you speed up the rate of people discovering how good your product is. When you have a bad product and go viral, you speed up the pace of people finding out that you sell a rubbish product. Fix your product first. Have a system in place to find deals that nobody else has. It's competitive out there; you need to protect your competitive edge.

When my social media audience started to grow, I knew my next step was to find more deals for my growing audience. I tried everything. My approach to business during those days was very, throw mud at the wall and see what sticks. I sent out a few deals each week and looked at what was popular with my audience. It definitely wasn't the smoothest approach, but it allowed me to see what worked and what didn't. This is how I created my strategy. Still, it took me 3 months from that very first video going viral to secure my first deal.

I sent out 50 deals and sold only 3 before I sat down to examine why this was the case. The more I sold, the more I noticed a pattern emerging. The properties that were selling were all:

- Under 100k
- Buy to Let
- Tenants in Place

My social following was made up of mainly working professionals who lived in the South of England. They wanted real estate with tenants in place so they could have a hands-off investment.

I had found the sweet spot for my business, so as all the business books I had read suggested, now that I had found something that worked, I did more of it. This is what helped me to scale so quickly, and I believe it is what helps all businesses scale quickly. Once you find what works, double down on it. You can continue to refine as you go along.

Soon, I became known for finding Buy to Let deals with tenants in place for under 100k. I had niched down on my social media, and all my content was educating people looking for those types of properties. I no longer had to go out and look for clients. They were finding me. This is the power of creating a niche.

A niche is your zone of expertise. When you have a niche, you are the go-to expert in a narrow field of focus. A common misconception is that you need to serve as many types of customers as possible to be successful. This will just make you a busy fool. It is difficult to market yourself in a way that will appeal to everyone. Different customer types have different needs.

When you have a niche, it is easier to create a service that is completely tailored to your ideal customer. It also makes it a lot easier to create content because you only have to cater to one type of customer. Don't be afraid to do things that others aren't doing because this will make you stand out. I don't think there are many other property sourcers out there dancing in front of the properties they've sold. It makes me stand out.

You may need to start off as a general property sourcer until you see what works but try to niche down as soon as you notice a pattern in the deals you sell. Look at the types of deals you are closing and who you are selling them to. The things that link all of these sales is your niche. I think the golden rule in business is once you find something that works well, do more of it. When you first start your business, this will prevent you from getting distracted by things that aren't profitable. Your niche could be a particular location, a property investment strategy, or even a customer type. If you want to get really specific, you could do all 3.

Now that I knew my audience and what they were looking for, I had to learn how to find the properties they wanted.

Where to Find Deals

There are two main ways to find deals for your clients:
1. On the market
2. Direct to Vendor

Direct to vendor is when you have exclusive access to a property because you are working directly with the seller. On the market deals are deals that almost anyone can find by working with an estate agent. They could even find these deals themselves on property portals if they put in a little bit of legwork. Let's start with the on market deals first.

On Market Deals

Property Portals

I found the house I was living in through property portals like Rightmove and Zoopla. So naturally, this is where I started.

The only issue with finding deals on property portals is that everyone has the same idea. You are not offering unique deals because this deal can be found by every other property sourcer out there. You aren't differentiating yourself; you're just one of many selling the same deal. If you do find deals on property portals, you need to be quick as the property portals are highly competitive marketplace getting millions of visitors each day.

Pros and Cons of Using Property Portals

Pros	Cons
● Easy to use • Well-laid out • Makes it easy to compare properties • Great market information and statistics	• Limited control • The client can find the deal themselves • More competition from buyers

The main issue I found with using property portals is that you have a lot less control over the deal. Your client can contact the seller or their agent directly, cutting you out of the deal. Learn from my mistakes and have a rock-solid contract in place if you find deals on property portals. This will stop clients from being able to cut you out of the deal.

I believe there is still a lot of value a property sourcer can offer a client with a deal they find on a property portal. You might secure the property for a lower price than listed (especially if it has been on Rightmove for a while without much interest) or even package the deal in a way that makes it more attractive to your target clients. As long as you are adding value for your client, then you are worth your fee.

I'm currently going through the process of purchasing a property portal deal! The value I added here is that it is advertised for £190,000, but I noticed it had been up for a long time on the portals. When a property has been up for a long time, naturally, people think there must be something wrong with it. After a bit of digging, the only issues with the property are that it was originally overpriced, and it needs some light modernising which is why it had been on Rightmove for so long.

I also found out that the vendor is a motivated seller on a deadline to get this sold. Long story short, I have negotiated a great deal far below market value and offered the vendor a very quick sale. So, you can find good deals on the property portals; you just have to think a bit differently from everyone else. This goes to show what is possible if you take the time to understand the vendors' biggest needs

- in this case, their priority was avoiding more time in the market. They were willing to reduce the sales price to achieve that.

Whether you use property portals to source deals or not, they are great resources to research the local area and offer comparables for my deals. Clients love these as they can see the value of the deal based on past sale prices and what is available in the local area.

Tip

If you are going to use property portals, you need to act quickly when a property hits the market. Turn notifications on to receive alerts when a deal matching your criteria hits Zoopla. This puts you in the best position to jump on the deal before everyone else sees it.

<u>Agents</u>

If you can build strong relationships with local estate agents, you can be the first person to hear about a new property. Estate agents don't have to be your competition; they can be your friends as a property sourcer. Think about it; they only collect a commission once they sell the property. By working with you, they increase the chances of selling the property quickly. Speak to all the local agents in the areas you are looking, tell them what you are looking for and ask them to let you know if something suitable comes up. They'll be likely to contact you about an opportunity before it hits the market. They want to close deals quickly just as much as you do.

Agents are specialists in their area, so they can be a wealth of information, especially when you are not familiar with a particular area. Lean on their experience and expertise, and you will gain a lot of insight into the area that you can pass on to your clients. They'll be able to provide you with information about local tenant profiles, expected rents, and market prices.

If you build a relationship with agents, they can sometimes also give you insight into the vendor's motivations. I had a real win early on because an agent gave me a heads-up that the vendor was looking for a quick sale and would be likely to accept £20k under asking. I took a look at the property and I secured an amazing deal. Buying below market value gives you a win before you have even started. To this day, I am so grateful that Ben helped me out.

Pros	**Cons**
• Local expertise	• On-market deals
• Insight into the vendor's state of mind	• They work on behalf of the seller

Auctions

Auctions are great places to find properties selling for a steal, especially if your clients don't mind renovating. Keep an eye on local auction catalogues to see what is coming up so you can see if they may be suitable for your clients. As with estate agents, if you nurture relationships with people at the auction houses, you might get advance notification of properties that would interest you or be able to book a private appointment to see the property with your client.

If you source property deals through auctions, make sure you have a strategy (and contract) in place to make sure your clients aren't disappointed or worse, you're left on the hook for the property. Also beware of the fees, because they can add up and can throw your numbers completely. Manage your clients' expectations and think about the best way to make auction sourcing work for all parties.

Off The Market Deals

Direct to vendor deals will set you apart as a property sourcer because you are able to get stock that your client would not be able to access themselves. You are providing your clients with extra value and lowering the risk of being cut out of the deal.

Direct to vendor deals are a win for the vendor too. They don't have to pay commissions or agency fees, and you can often find them a buyer quicker with less disruption (no open houses or a parade of unqualified buyers.) You can use the savings to leverage a great deal for your clients and create a win-win all around.

Now you may be asking how to go about this, and this is what we will run through. As a property sourcer, I feel I have tried every trick in the book, some are more successful than others, but a diverse approach will ensure that you always have a pipeline of stock and you never struggle to find opportunities for your clients. Without opportunities, your business quickly grinds to a halt. So, mastering a few key routes to vendors will help you build your reputation.

As you get better at your deal-finding, people will start coming to you, and you won't need to work so hard to find deals. We have people getting in touch with us to tell us about their property and ask if we would have investors. That is something I never could've foreseen when I started KO Estates. It is all because we built great relationships and consistently delivered on our promises. Create a situation where everyone wins, and it will be easy to scale.

<u>Lettering</u>

I use this method a lot in my business. I send letters to owners of properties that match my needs asking them to consider selling. It's a win-win because the seller gets a quick sale without having to pay estate agent fees, and you get an off-market deal for your clients.

The best approach is to ask them if they are open to a conversation. Do not mention actual numbers in the initial contact, just that you could get a good offer for them. You do not have enough information to give a price indication at this stage. You need to see inside and get a good idea of the condition and size of the property. The goal of this contact is to spark the idea in their mind. If they get in touch to learn more, you can take it from there.

It is easy to get excited when you get a lead with direct vendor lettering. But don't price in order to make it work. You need to determine what number would work for you and your investors and stick to that number. If the numbers don't work for the seller, then move on. There are always more deals out there. Just be polite and honest with the vendor that the number they are looking for does not work for you. The best piece of advice I can give you in property sourcing is to know when to walk away.

Pros	**Cons**
● More control of the deal	● Expense of printing the letters

• More time to sell the deal • Build a relationship with the seller that could result in referrals or future deals • The seller avoids agent fees	• It takes time to deliver the letters • Long-term strategy, it often takes 3-6 months for people to get back to you • Manual process

At times I feel crazy writing letters; my generation is all about digital communication. I think that's why it works. People are bombarded with emails and text messages, so a letter stands out. People also get excited to see a letter that is not a bill coming through their door. It is less likely to be ignored.

Tip

This strategy works best at scale because you are going to get more nos (or no response at all) than yes. But if you get 1 out of 100, it will be worth it for the off-market deals. Clients love exclusivity.

Time is money, so even though handwritten letters look more personal. Don't hand write every single letter. I recommend either photocopying a handwritten letter or typing your letter. This will allow you to mass-print them.

Use the link below to grab an example of this letter, this letter has had phenomenal success, now it's yours but keep me posted on your success with it!

www.property-sourcing-secrets.com/vendorletter

As your business grows, you could hire a company to write and deliver these letters for you. This service costs, but it will save you a lot of time.

Make sure you have a system in place to track who you have sent letters to and who has responded so you don't inundate anyone with multiple letters. It can also give you a list of people to follow up with.

<u>Your Network</u>

Tell EVERYONE what you do. It sounds simple, but the people you already know can help you find deals or investors. Even if the people in your life don't need your services, they may know someone who does.

I secured a portfolio of properties that had a £100,000 sourcing fee attached because someone I knew passed on my details to someone they knew. You will be surprised at the connections you make and the doors that will open by telling people what you do.

Pros	**Cons**
● Free	● You need to get over shyness or nerves to do this
● Easy to do	

I find myself doing this naturally because I love what I do and really enjoy chatting about it.

Social Media

This is another way to tell people what you do on a much larger scale. My social media allows me to reach a global audience to tell them what I do and show the results. I meet investors and find deals through my social media. People will see what you do and get in touch if your interests align.

I have an "Ask and you shall receive" policy when it comes to my social media. If I am looking for new stock, I tell my audience I am looking for new stock and ask them to get in touch if they know of anything. Do this from a place of adding value and helping your audience.

Pros	Cons
● Free advertising ● Global reach	● Need to build trust with your audience

Tip

Work with other deal sourcers when you are starting out. Not only can you share deals and clients, only one of you needs to meet compliance requirements.

Property Professionals

Imagine you are a landowner or own a property that needs a little bit of development to reach its potential. Where is the first place you would go? You would call an architect!

Architects see thousands of opportunities because they are the expert called in to advise property owners. They speak directly to the owners and give their expert advice. Architects are great connections to have!

When I first started, I didn't have any architects in my circle, but with a little bit of networking, I now know plenty. You have to put the legwork in to make these valuable connections. LinkedIn is a great place to start because you can find people by job title and location. Use the filters to create a list of hand-picked connections.

Networking is a long-term game. It is all about building a relationship, not selling. The aim is to build trust and likeability. Sometime in the future, you may be able to mutually benefit each other.

If you go in with the intention to sell from the start, you will push people away. Do you respond to the cold sales messages you get on LinkedIn or social media?

HMO Register

If your investors want a HMO (House of Multiple Occupancy), then this is a great technique. All owners of HMOs need to be on the HMO register by law. This is a ready-made contact list for you to send direct to vendor letters. You never know; you may catch someone on the right day and make a deal.

Pros	Cons
● Ready-made list	● Only works for HMOs
● Same as direct to vendor	● Same as direct to vendor

You can take two approaches in a direct to vendor sale. The first is talking directly to the vendor, and the second is using an agent portal to speak to the vendor. I have tried using agent portals, but it is much harder because you have a lot less control. Communicating over an agent portal can be frustrating for the vendors, so you have to work a lot harder to build the relationship and establish trust. For me, it was not worth it. I recommend just approaching the vendor directly. Try and talk to them over the phone, by email, or in person.

Deal Sourcers

Don't look at other deal sourcers like your competition. They can actually be your biggest asset.

Collaborating with others grows the opportunities for both of you and expands your resources. You get access to their clients, and they get access to yours. Win-win.

If the result is that you serve your customers better, then it will improve your business.

During my first year in business, I organically built a database of 12,000 investors. Sounds great, right? However, it is a lot of people looking for a property. And once I niched down, not every investor in my database was looking for the type of properties I specialise in. Some customers want a particular type of property or location.

When I work with other deal sourcers, I can help the investors on my list find their deals. I can also get deals or clients from the other deal sourcer's list. Collaborations have allowed me to sell deals I would not otherwise be able to and have allowed me to reach new people.

Usually, the sourcing fee is split between the two parties; you each bring something of value to the table. I see many property sourcers that get put off by the reduced sourcing fee. But instead of seeing it as a reduced fee, look at it as an extra fee you gained because you would not have been able to serve that client without the collaboration.

At KO Estates, we partner with lots of property sourcers. It is one of our scaling tactics. We see this as a partnership where the property sourcers we work with grow as we do. They bring us deals, and we find an investor that suits the deal. This is another reason why I started the Sourcing Secrets programme. By training other property sourcers, I can ensure the people we partner with will treat our clients or vendors as well as we would. Deal sourcers in our programme start their business with a powerful network of our partners. I will leave all the links you need to join our programmes at the back of the book.

Pros	Cons
● More opportunities • Database sharing • Building a network • Increasing brand awareness • Splitting the workload	

There are so many different weird and wonderful ways you can find deals; you are only limited by your imagination and determination. I recommend trying all of these techniques and seeing what you prefer. Some of these techniques have brought me more success than others, but I never rely solely on one option. Diversifying the way you find deals means that you will always have a pipeline of deals for your clients.

Once you establish yourself, people will start contacting you with deals to sell, both other property sourcers and vendors. It's crazy. At KO Estates, we get so many inbound deals (that's what we call them) that we actually say no to the majority of messages. That's not because we don't want to sell properties, obviously, we do; it's just that we have a reputation to uphold. Our clients expect a certain type of property from us and crazy good deals, so we only promote deals that fit our parameters. Good deals and good stock are the foundation of our business. If we can consistently deliver good deals, then we will never have an issue scaling our business.

The main theme of all the methods is talking to people, networking and seeing what can be done. You will be amazed at how many good deals basically fall into your lap once you have these conversations. I've had people connect me with someone who had a deal or contact me when they were ready to sell because they remembered the conversation that we had a few months ago.

Don't overwhelm yourself by trying to do everything at once. Choose one method to try at a time. Give it your all and track results so you can see what works and what doesn't.

Go and Do It

Finding deals that wow your customer requires a little bit of legwork. Remember, property sourcing is a long game, so the contacts you are making today will pay off in 6-12 months. Don't get discouraged if you don't see any immediate benefit to your efforts. Here are some good places to start:

- Property portals like Rightmove or Zoopla – Remember your clients have access to these portals, too, so you need to be smart if you use these.
- Direct to vendor lettering – Post letters to properties that meet your requirements and ask them to contact you if they are interested in selling their property.
- Your network – Talk about what you do to the people you know. You never know what kind of contacts your friends and family have.
- Social media – Share what you do on social media and reach a global audience.
- Property professionals – Get to know property professionals in your area. You will need a network of builders, architects, mortgage advisors, and solicitors anyway, and they might recommend you to their clients.
- HMO register – If you source deals for HMOs, the HMO register provides a list of current HMO owners.
- Other property sourcers – Connect with property sourcers in other niches. You may be able to work together on deals where you both bring value to the table.

How to Approach Deals

Once you've come across a good deal, you need to evaluate the deal to see if it will work for your investors. There are a lot of good deals out there, but just because something is a good deal, doesn't mean it's right for your investors. Here is how I evaluate the deals I find.

Deal Review

Good deals don't hang around. Reviewing the numbers is a great way to quickly and accurately see if a deal will work for our clients before we spend time on a deal. Read this section carefully because understanding the numbers behind a deal is extremely important. This is where so many deal sourcers go wrong. They promote a deal to their clients without running the figures and end up promoting bad deals. That will erode the trust you have worked so hard to build with your clients. Run the numbers before you promote anything. Make sure you are presenting a fantastic money-making opportunity on a silver platter. The best way to do that is to look at ROI.

ROI stands for return on investment, and it is basically telling you how much profit your investor will make if they purchase the property. This is super easy for flip projects; just divide the profit by the amount invested. Let's say your client invested £120,000 in a property flip and made a profit of £30,000. To calculate the ROI, divide the profit by the investment. £30,000 divided by £120,000 is 25%.

To calculate the ROI for a B2L (Buy to Let) property, we talk about yield. Yield percentage = the annual rental income divided by the total property price. Let's say your client buys a £95,000 property that generates £700 per month in rental income. First, you need to calculate how much rent the property earns each year. £700 x 12 = £8,400. Then, divide £8,400 by £95,000 = 8% yield.

Keep in mind that these examples look at gross profit numbers and don't account for the fees or monthly expenses of owning a property. For example, a B2L property owner will need to put money aside for repairs, property taxes, and agency fees.

Net figures are used to demonstrate to clients what they take home at the end of each month after all expenses. This is an important detail to include when presenting the deal to clients and comparing deals. To really compare apples with apples, you need to work in net figures because that will leave you with the exact profit as opposed to inflated figures. I have a spreadsheet that I use to run the numbers on deals. That way, I know every fee and charge is accounted for and this gives me confidence that my figures will work for my clients.

If the deal checks out and the numbers look good, then we can then crack on with our due diligence process and arrange a viewing.

Viewings

When I bought my own place, I didn't use viewings effectively at all. I poked around the house and got distracted chatting with the estate agent. I came out of the viewing none the wiser of any of the important and potentially costly elements of the property. Yet I put in an offer on the same day as that ineffective viewing. Thinking back, it is crazy to think I spent my life savings on something after only a 10-minute viewing. I spend way more time looking when I buy a pair of shoes, and they're nowhere near the same price category as real estate. I was lucky, and none of those came back to bite me. (I don't want to jinx it, but so far, so good)

Having other people spend considerable amounts of money based on my recommendations was a wake-up call. I was conducting viewings to see if the property was worth recommending to my clients. I wanted to be able to show that I left no stone unturned. I also wanted a reputation for only bringing high-quality deals to my clients.

I will never sell anything that I or my team has not viewed. But it is not enough to simply enter the property; you need to find answers to all your questions.

It is easy to get distracted when you are on a viewing. When I first started, I would be busy chatting with the estate agent or vendor and forget to get the details I needed for my deal review. I would be left with questions and forget the details I did get. It is not a bad thing to chat with the estate agent, they are great connections to have, and if they like you, they are more likely to help you reach a favourable outcome. However, you need to assess the deal too.

I decided I needed to put a process in place to make these viewings more effective. So, I created a viewing checklist to prompt me to look for key details and make sure I got all the information I need. The checklist keeps me focused and is there to make sure I don't forget anything.

Head to the link below to download my viewing checklist for your next viewings.

www.property-sourcing-secrets.com/viewing-checklist

As you work through the checklist, you may notice some issues with the property. Don't worry if you do find issues. It is great that you caught the issue, and there is no problem that can't be fixed. Some investors on your list won't mind putting a little work in; you just need to make sure the price reflects the amount of work needed. You can use the things you noticed as a negotiation technique.

Problems or issues with the property offer an opportunity to add value to the property. For example, if the boiler is about to go, it could cost around £2,500 to get a new one. You need to factor this into your calculations so that the price reflects the extra work. The property owner would need to pay for the boiler anyway if they don't sell the property, so it is standard to factor the price into the sale price.

The issues you find will help you justify your offer. They show your logic so you don't seem like you're making a cheeky offer. Justifying your offer opens up a reasonable conversation.

Builder Quotes

When I first started as a property sourcer, I asked 3 builders to look at the property with me and give me a quote. Every single time I would receive 3 very different quotes.

I attended a course by Paul Tickner and it opened my eyes to a more effective way of doing things. The reason I was getting such different quotes was because I was leaving a lot up to interpretation.

Paul Tickner suggests being more specific. Before, I would say, "I want to redo the bathroom." This could result in a quote anywhere from £150 to £10,000 because there is a lot of room for interpretation. Do I want to redo the tiles? Do I want to keep the current fixtures and fittings?

List exactly what you want to change in each room and ask the builders for a clear, itemised quote so you can provide your clients with that information when presenting the deal. Be clear about the standard you want and the types of materials, so there is no confusion for the builder or your clients. Everyone is on the same page and understands what the quote is for. Taking this approach will save you a lot of time and effort. It did for my business.

Negotiation

You need to have a love of numbers for this line of work. Investing is a numbers game, and you need to be unemotional and focused on the numbers in order to be successful. At the start, it is so easy to become excited by a deal and sacrifice your profit in the name of making the deal work.

Anyone can be the highest bidder in the room, but that approach is not effective, and it will not serve your customers. Before I enter a negotiation, I go back to my niche, my deal criteria, my clients' wants and needs to make this deal work. My client has to be front of mind the entire time because if it doesn't meet their needs, then I will struggle to sell the deal.

For example, my investors may want a minimum of 7% yield on a Buy to Let (B2L). With that in mind, I work out the very top figure

I could offer on that particular deal in order to meet the criteria (the 7% yield).

Armed with this information, I then know exactly when to walk away, and that's important. It's so easy to get wrapped up in the excitement of negotiation and think it's only another £1,000. Before you know it, you are £10,000 over budget, which means you will struggle to sell the deal. So, knowing the highest possible figure is going to keep us safe. It's also going to confirm when a deal is good and give us a rule of thumb to go by throughout the negotiation on that property. If you can't secure it for that price or lower, walk away. Move on instead of wasting more time on the deal. Knowing when to walk away is one of the most important negotiating skills.

There are two main negotiating styles I use depending on the property and circumstances.

Low blow

This is the negotiating style most people are familiar with. You make a first offer that leaves considerable room for negotiation before you hit your top figure. The vendor then counters, and you negotiate until either you find a figure that works for both of you or you walk away. Typically, a vendor may want to meet you halfway, so just make sure that if they do, that figure would still be lower than your top figure.

Don't allow yourself to get pulled into a bidding war during negotiations. Keep your top figure in mind and walk away from the deal if it hits that figure. Remember, if you go over your top figure, the deal is useless to you because your investors are unlikely to want it.

When you use the low blow strategy, expect people to say no. If you are not hearing no, then you are not going in low enough. Some vendors will be in a position to go for a low offer because their property has been on the market for some time. Sometimes, they just want a quick sale.

Increase the number of low blow offers you are making. This is a little bit of a scattergun approach. You are not legally bound to the sale at this stage; you are just securing the price. Don't be afraid to be a little cheeky here. Some people are better at this than others, but you have a job to do. It can help to detach your emotions here. Remember who you serve. Your clients are coming to you for low prices, so you are negotiating on their behalf. Vendors will look out for their own interests; they will tell you if your offer is too low, and you can go from there.

Last and Final

This is a great negotiation tactic if competition is high, like an on market deal. You don't play games; you just tell them this is my last and final offer (sometimes also called best and final offer) and see if they accept it or not.

I say something like this. "This is my only and final offer. I won't negotiate; if it works, then great, and if not, then I'll have to walk away. I would like to offer XXX. I'm in a position where I am ready to go and can complete in XX days. (If you are a cash buyer, mention this too because it will sweeten the deal.)

Calculate the top figure for your last and final offer. Going back to that previous example of 7%, I would work out the very top figure that would secure the 7% yield for the client and offer that. The best thing about a last and final is all your cards are on the table. You cannot go any higher as it would go above the threshold that would work for clients. If your offer is not accepted, then you know you couldn't have done any more.

Remember, price is not always the only thing the vendor is looking for. Contingencies and timeframes are valuable parts of the negotiation and could be higher priorities than price, especially in unfortunate circumstances like divorce, rebate, and death. In these circumstances, £10,000 won't change their life; they are more concerned with their time. This is why it's key to understand the vendor's motivation. To swing a last and final offer, we want the vendor to feel like they are winning. When we know their situation, we know what we can offer to set us apart from other buyers. That is a powerful thing in a negotiation.

A great example of this is when my mum made an offer on a property that she had fallen in love with. It was out of her price range, but she worked out what figure she could make work and made an offer. That vendor had 5 offers made on the same day to compare. My mum's offer was not the highest offer, but when she sent it, she said that she had already sold her house, so she would be able to move quickly. If you have ever had a sale fall through because of an onward chain, then you know it is worth taking a slightly lower offer. In this case, the vendor was selling the property to fund building their own house. The plan to build their house would come crashing down if they didn't get the cash and quick. If you understand the needs of the vendor, then you won't have to worry about the pricing.

Go and Do It

You have to take a volume approach to scale your business. You will not win every deal, so you need to create a pipeline full of deals. This will help you to not get too emotionally invested in individual deals.

The more offers you make, the closer you will get to a result. As long as you know your walk away figure, you are safe here; work that out first for every deal and go into negotiations with confidence. If that one doesn't work, there will be one that does. Every offer you make and every negotiation you enter will help you learn. The more offers you make, the better you will get.

I also want you to be confident that you can walk away if the number creeps above your top figure. There will be a deal out there that does stack up.

Once you have a possible deal, you need to evaluate the quality before you can even think about presenting it to your clients. There are 3 steps to this process:

1. Deal Review – Check if the numbers work before you spend time on due diligence. If it is a property flip, calculate the ROI. If it is a B2L (Buy to Let) deal, calculate the yield. Use these numbers to see if the deal is right for your investors.
2. Viewings – Follow a viewing checklist so you don't miss anything. Look for any issues that require work. You can use this in negotiations to get a better price. Your clients

will appreciate having a detailed summary of the work needed on the property.
3. Builder's Quotes – Be specific about what you want to change and ask the builder for an itemised quote. You can lean on the builder's expertise too. Have a conversation about how to create the most value in the property and ask them to provide an itemised quote.
4. Negotiation – Work out the numbers you need on the property and speak to the owner to see what their numbers are. You may need to negotiate a little to find a deal that works for both of you. Know your maximum price and be prepared to walk away from the deal if it doesn't meet your needs.

How to Find Investors

Once we have a deal, we need someone to sell that deal to. Finding investors starts with putting yourself out there and sharing what you do. Talk about what you do everywhere you possibly can and get people excited about what you offer. This is your first touchpoint with potential investors, so you need to get them excited about your deals and show that you can provide the expertise they need.

I recommend starting with free ways of getting yourself out there and building a list of investors. This will help you keep costs low while you are refining your niche and making your first few deals. Some free methods of finding investors we will discuss are social media, email lists, and being featured in publications. You could also use paid advertising to accelerate your process if you would like. Paid methods of finding investors are not necessary for your success. I started KO Estates and scaled it using the free methods in this chapter.

Social Media

One of the biggest fears the property sourcers I coach have is whether they will be able to find people to buy their deals.

I'm here to tell you we have access to virtually everyone in the world for free, all from our phones; we just have to make sure we are reaching the right people. We live in a time of incredible opportunity because of social media. 10-20 years ago, I would not have been able to scale KO Estates as quickly as I did because social media didn't exist as it does today. It would have taken a lot more work to reach people.

Social media offers free marketing, and if you are not using it, you are putting yourself at a disadvantage. That is true no matter what industry you are in. The great news for you is that social media is massively underutilised in the UK property market, so you are far ahead of anyone else. A lot of Highstreet agents either don't have Instagram or have a really poor Instagram account. They rely on word of mouth and their Highstreet presence.

These tactics have limited success, but social media is unbelievably powerful. I sold over 100 deals in a year just by using social media. No paid ads, no paid media, just me and my iPhone. I think some agents are missing out on the potential.

When I started, social media was my only option because I had no money. I couldn't afford ad campaigns or billboards. I had to find a free method to attract clients. I use social media a lot, not just to keep up with friends but to purchase items like clothes and gym leggings. So, I thought what's to say people wouldn't buy property on social media?

Over time, I saw that I could use my social media to create an unlimited number of leads for my business, all for free. It was really cool, and I just assumed everyone was doing the same thing as me. It wasn't until I started speaking to other people in the industry that I realised how special this was. Other property sourcers and estate agents were paying a lot for leads, and their ad campaigns were bringing in a small number of customers. My free marketing strategy was creating thousands of leads per month. The expressions on their faces when I told them what I was doing were priceless. They were not marketing in the same way I was, but they soon wanted to!

The Power of Social Media

I am not on Twitter and have not actively used it to grow KO Estates so far. (Never say never) That being said, KO Estates and I were trending on Twitter back in April 2021. *Katie, I thought you said you didn't have Twitter?* That was exactly what I thought.

A magazine emailed me asking if they could interview me because of a trending tweet related to me. I thanked them for getting in touch but told them they must be mistaken. It couldn't be me because I was not on Twitter.

I told my brother about the conversation, mentioning it was so weird that this happened. He did a quick search and found the thread the journalist was talking about. He suggested that I shouldn't read the thread. Well, I don't know about you, but whenever someone says I shouldn't read something, I of course want to read it. So, onto Twitter I went!

Someone had screenshotted a reel I created explaining the rental income you could receive from owning a particular property. This had somehow sparked a national discussion about whether it was ethical to own a property to rent. A lot of people agreed, and a lot of people disagreed. It got people talking.

I see a lot of people who really hold back on social media because they are afraid of things like this. They are worried that they will face criticism. My brother warned me against reading the Twitter thread because he was worried that I would be hurt by the criticism. I know not everyone feels this way, but I don't mind the negative comments. People are entitled to their own opinions, and the more people discuss their opinions, the more exposure KO Estates was getting.

Not everyone is going to agree with owning property to rent (I'm not sure why, everyone needs a place to live, and not everyone can afford to buy), but I don't care about the opinions of those people because they are unlikely to be my customers. Remember, I find deals solely for Buy to Let investors. So, if they're not looking to buy a rental property, they're not my clients.

My clients are the people whose opinions matter most. As long as I am serving them and getting them results, I am happy. It is impossible to please everyone, so focus on the people you are serving. If you don't make your clients happy, you don't have a business.

In a weird way, I am grateful for every negative tweet in that Twitter thread. They helped me to reach new people on a social media platform I am not even on. I have clients who saw that thread and got in touch because they liked what they saw. Those are clients I got with absolutely zero work; thank you, negative Twitter people! People would kill to get that level of exposure!

There are always going to be people who have something negative to say, no matter what you do. Your first priority needs to be your business. In order to get more exposure for your business, you need to put yourself out there more.

Social Media Platforms

Here is a brief recap of each social media platform and the demographics that use it as of today when writing this. Social Media is an ever changing world so imagine this will not be accurate for long.

- **TikTok** – Started as a younger crowd, but it is now an established platform. TikTok empowers content creators and makes it easier than any other social media platform to get in front of a large audience. Financial education and investment content do really well on TikTok.
- **Instagram** – One of the most used apps. It is popular with a large range of demographics. I think Instagram works really well with properties because it is such a visual platform. At the moment, Instagram is really pushing Reels which are short videos similar to TikTok.
- **Facebook** – Facebook groups are fantastic for building a sense of community and encouraging your audience to learn and grow together.
- **LinkedIn** – A different type of audience, LinkedIn is a more professional social media platform. It is a great place to build a network of other property professionals and landlords because you can search based on location and job title.
- **YouTube** – Long-form video content. YouTube is owned by Google, so popular topical videos will display in Google search results.

- **Twitter** – A great way to join conversations and meet new people. Journalists hang out a lot on Twitter, so it can be a great way to get media coverage.

How to Have the Most Impact on Social Media

Being successful on social media is easier said than done. I recommend taking the time to review your analytics on a regular basis so you can refine your strategy and work smart rather than hard. Here are some tips to get you started.

INSTAGRAM JAN 2020:

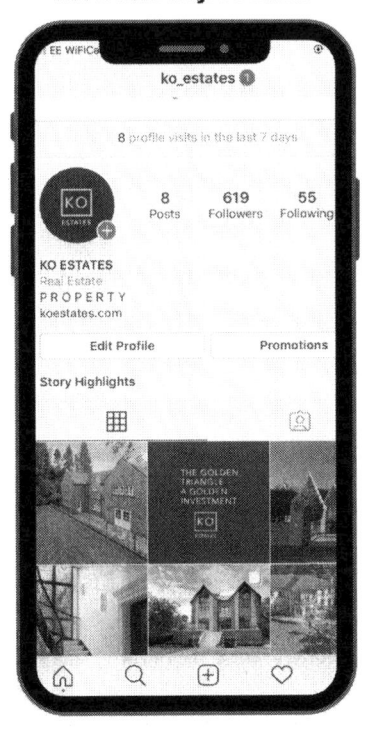

INSTAGRAM TODAY:

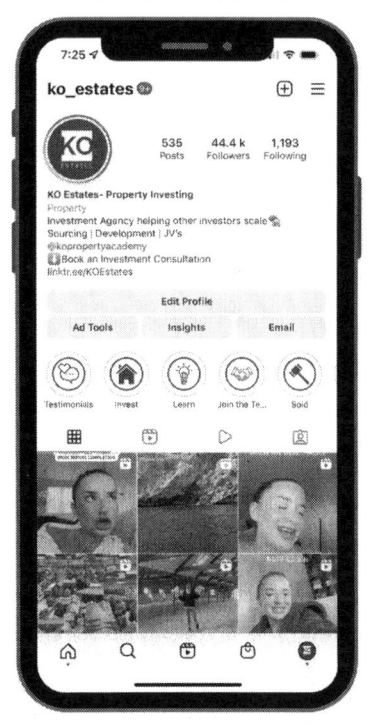

Here is the KO Estates Growth in about a year. We started like everyone with 0 followers but I built it up day by day here are some of the things I learnt throughout this process.

Consistent Posting Schedule

This is advice you will hear from anyone talking about how to grow your social media following. It is good advice, so it bears repeating. The people who do really well on social media post every day, often 3 times per day. That can seem like a lot when you're first starting out, but it keeps you fresh in your followers' minds.

Social media has been really powerful in growing KO Estates. It is not unusual for me to get around 10 messages a week on Instagram from people saying they have between £25k- £250k available and want me to help them find an investment property. These are organic leads that found me with zero ad spend. Social media is free marketing. To me, it is a no-brainer to use it as much as possible. It truly is one of those things where the more you put in, the better your results. Social media platforms want more people to use the platforms for longer. That is how they get the numbers to sell their ads. So, it makes logical sense that they reward accounts that achieve both quality and quantity.

I still manage my social media account myself on top of my own busy work schedule and there are two techniques I use to post multiple times a day.

1. Batching – I plan and create my content ahead of time. Sometimes a week ahead or up to a month ahead of time, depending on the type of content. This means I always have something to post, and I'm not scrambling to put

something out there. I can concentrate on making my content when I have something quality to share.
2. Repurposing content – Don't be afraid to repost old posts again. Your new audience may not have seen the post before, or it may be relevant again due to recent events. If you post on YouTube or have a blog, you can also take snippets from this long-form content to post on your social media platforms. This is great for when you are struggling for ideas or when you want to drive traffic to your other forms of content.

Add Value

You want to give away as much value to your clients at every stage. This starts with your social media presence all the way through to the packaged deal you offer. When you add value and go the extra mile, you stand out from your competition. People see that you really care about them, that you're not just in it for the money.

Creating valuable content serves two purposes:

1. It strengthens your brand
2. It attracts the right clients

Your content needs to be catered toward the type of clients you want to serve, aka your niche. If you are sourcing land deals, there is no point in building a list of hands-off first-time investors. They won't want what you are selling.

So, create the type of content your ideal client will find valuable.

Each post you create should fulfil a purpose. My social media posts for KO Estates have to hit at least one of these 4 purposes:

- Educate – provide my audience with knowledge
- Entertain – something fun related to the topic
- Inspire – show the possibilities to get my clients excited
- Convert – sell an offer

Ask yourself what your target clients want to see from you, or better yet, ask them! Use polls to ask your followers what information they want to see and how you can best serve them. They will be all too happy to tell you. Make sure you save responses for future content ideas!

At KO Estates, we spend a lot of time educating our social media audience, and while we promote deals frequently, it is a small percentage of our posts. By spending a lot of time educating our audience on property investing, we build a lot of trust and prime clients to work with us. Recently we sold some properties in Blackpool, and while we were preparing the deals, we posted a lot about the Blackpool area, what to look for in property, and typical rental values in the area. Once we had educated our audience and given them value, then we showed them the deals.

By serving before we sell, our clients have learned something from our posts, so no matter the outcome, they win. We grow our audience because they want to learn from us, not because they want to be constantly sold to. Once they're following us, they are picking up property investment tips, seeing the wins we get for other clients, and then when they are ready, they are perfectly positioned to jump on a deal we promote. Don't think of social media as an advertising platform; no one likes being sold to. Instead, use it to provide value, and you will capture and keep your followers' attention.

Viral Posts

The first time I went viral was completely by accident, but I have since managed to go viral a few times on purpose too. From those experiences, I have found the elements of a viral post so I can replicate the process again and again. Now, my Instagram account has reached 1.5 million accounts per month FOR FREE.

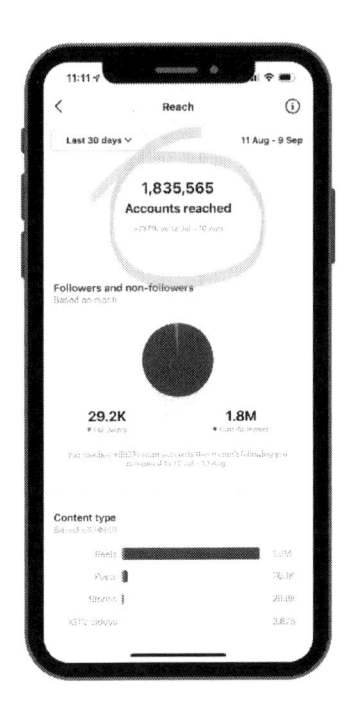

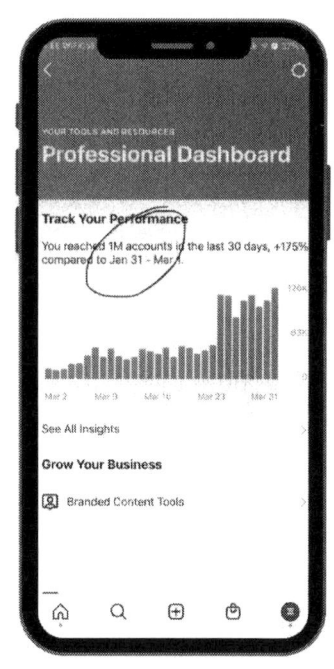

These are the elements of a viral social media post:

- **Numbers** – People love seeing the numbers behind something. It also adds a level of authenticity if they can see the numbers behind the passive income. This can get people excited
- **Face** – People connect with people, so show your face. By doing this, you give them someone they can know, like, and trust. We'll talk about this more in a bit when we discuss personal brand.
- **Short and snappy** – Aside from YouTube, social media is all about micro-content. Break things down into small bite-sized pieces.
- **Feel good** – People love feel-good content. Think of the social media content you enjoy most; they all have that positive, feel-good energy.
- **Attention-grabbing** – You need to grab attention to stop the scrolling. Have a hook within the first 3 seconds to make sure people stick around to consume your content.
- **Call to Action** - Tell your audience what to do next at the end of each post. Adding a call to action increases engagement with your posts because you are inviting viewers to interact with you. Engagement is key in social media because platform algorithms reward profiles with high engagement. Your posts will be shown to a wider pool of viewers because engagement is the sign of good content. At the end of the day, it's called SOCIAL media; it's designed to be a two-way conversation, so engage with your followers and encourage them to engage with you.

Common calls to action are "comment and tell me your thoughts on X," or "tag a friend who needs to hear this." You could even invite people to message you to discuss a property deal.

- **Partner with Others** - A great way to take the pressure off yourself is to interview others. This will help you to build up your confidence and help you to reach more people by sharing your audiences.

Personal Brand

Personal brand is a buzzword you have probably already heard. If you haven't it is about marketing yourself in a way that emphasises the personality traits your audience will connect with. Corporate personal branding might emphasise professionalism and expertise. Personal branding can also be a little more casual and showcase your personality, like mine does. The one thing that all personal branding needs is your face.

You are marketing yourself as an expert, the go-to person for your niche. By showing what you do behind the scenes and documenting your process. You become more relatable, more approachable, and people find it easier to connect with you.

Think about the influencers you follow online. You see their lives every day and start to feel like you know them as well as you know your friends. This is what you need to do with your brand. Be you every time you show up online, dorky sense of humour and all. It is much easier for people to connect with your personal brand when they see you as a real human being. Don't be afraid to share your mistakes or make a terrible pun.

Most people choose to go faceless on their Instagram so that they can stay anonymous. This is how I started out, so I get it, but people struggle to connect with faceless brands. Without connection, there is no loyalty. Putting a face to your brand helps to make your brand relatable and allows you to build trust with your audience.

Mindset

It can feel embarrassing and overwhelming to get started on social media. And the main thing that stops people from getting started in social media is mainly the fear of what other people will think. Public criticism is up there too! I get it because when I started, I was the same too. I remember feeling so vulnerable putting myself out there.

I was listening to podcasts and reading business books that all told me how important social media was, but I still wasn't doing it. It is one thing to know you have to do something, and it is another to do it.

What snapped me out of this was looking at my account and realising it was not getting much traction. I asked myself what was more embarrassing, the failing account or me failing to try? I was holding myself back from success because I was not putting the effort in. So, I decided I needed to give it a proper go.

I can confirm that this was the best decision I had ever made. Posts with my face performed far better than posts without my face. It didn't matter the topic or content; posts with my face always won, sometimes a thousand times over. Give your following a real person to connect with. You will become more relatable and trustworthy because you are putting a face to what you do.

And the best thing is, when you first start out, you will not have many followers for your first few weeks and months. This is good news. It gives you time to try things in relative privacy and get all the bad content out of the way before you attract a global audience. I laugh and sometimes cringe at my early posts now. Nobody posts A+ content from the very start; there is a learning curve to social media.

I am grateful for those early posts, as cringeworthy as they are, because they helped me to build momentum. Without them, I wouldn't be where I am today. I'm sorry to tell you that everyone has to go through that awkward phase. I can assure you there are good times ahead. These awkward posts are the foundations of your future. Celebrate them!

The best advice I can give you about getting started on social media is don't let other people stop you from achieving your goals.

At the start, you are not going to be good. Expect it. No one expects you to have it all figured out on day 1. People may point this out to you. Ignore them. You may compare yourself to other people. Stop it. Those people have been doing this a lot longer than you have. This may not even be their first social media account. You cannot compete with people who have been doing this for years from day one. Focus on building your audience and creating content that works for your niche.

Don't wait to be perfect to start. You need to throw yourself into the deep end and learn on the job. I am still learning. I find new ways to improve my social media content and engage with my audience all the time.

Limiting beliefs will hold you back if you let them. You have to focus on what you want. Are you more afraid of failing or more afraid of letting fear stop you from reaching your potential?

Everyone who puts content on the internet cringes at their early work, but cringey work is far better than having no work because you never started.

"You don't have to be great to start, but you have to start to be great"

– Zig Ziglar.

The results are so powerful. Commit to 30 days and test for yourself: it's going to be your favourite tool when clients are forming an orderly queue for your deals. Get this right, and you can sell a deal in seconds!

Email List

When I started KO Estates, I was lucky to have a friend who doubled as a mentor to me. He gave me some great advice early doors. While I was building my following on social media, Steve explained how important an email list is. I didn't realise at the time how crucial it was; I thought email was a little archaic when it comes to reaching clients, but I went along with it anyway, and I am so glad I did. Thank you, Steve! Now it's my turn to pass on that advice to you.

I can't stress enough how important email lists are. A social media audience is amazing, but what if Instagram goes down or your account is hacked? Social media allows you to reach a large global audience. But the downside is you have no control over it. A change to the algorithm of your social media platform could mean your followers no longer see your content. If your business relies solely upon Instagram, then your business success is at the whim of the people in Instagram head office.

Having a website and an email list means that no matter what happens, you still have access to your clients. You can still serve them and send them deals. The people who sign up for your email list are likely to be warm leads. They have already bought from you, downloaded a free product, or they want to hear more from you.

On the 4th of October, Meta's social media platforms went down. Facebook, WhatsApp, and Instagram all went down. Businesses lost billions in revenue that day. They had no way to sell to clients or find new clients.

I was still able to sell my deals on that day. Why? Because I had spent a lot of time growing my email list. My email list gives me direct contact with my client. No matter what happens with social media or the algorithms, I can show up for my community.

In the first year, I built a list of about 13,000 clients. I thought that was ok, but I didn't have any previous experience in this game. I wasn't sure how big my email list should be because I had nothing to compare it to. It wasn't until I spoke to others that I realised I was killing it. People were amazed that I had 13,000 people on my email list after less than a year in business. Their next question was always, "can you show me how?"

A lot of other agents were using Rightmove to find their clients and spending thousands of pounds a month to do so. They said that each lead would cost them £50 on average. Here I was, making thousands a month without spending anything. The process I was using can be set up in a day without any technical knowledge.

I had no ad spend, so I had no other option than to work this out and create this list organically.

Like every first-time entrepreneur, I started with 0 followers and no money to spend on ads. I had to grow my following and email list organically. Everyone has to start somewhere. In 2 months, I built a list of 1,000 investors. When I launched my Sourcing Secrets programme, I had to start from scratch again because my email list was full of property investors, not aspiring property sourcers. I followed the same method I teach in my course and had 600 aspiring property sourcers on my list within a week. The formula is replicable and will fill your list with ideal clients screaming for your property deals.

An email list is your most valuable business asset, as people are giving you closer access to them in exchange for value. The way most business owners (including me) provide value is through a lead magnet.

Lead Magnets

I don't know about you, but I avoid signing up for email lists at all costs because I don't want to be bombarded with spam emails. My inbox is cluttered enough. I don't need more unwanted emails. A lot of people feel the same way, which is why we offer something in exchange for their email addresses.

A freebie.

This is a hack to help you grow your email list and produce a large list of leads to grow your investor list. You give your client something of value in return for their email address. It provides a win-win. Your clients get something they want, and you get their email address. They are more likely to give their email address because you are offering something they want.

You need to offer the right kind of freebie in order to attract the right people. You want to fill your email list with your ideal customers. If your niche targets professional investors, you could offer a market update as a freebie. These types of investors want to see the growth of their investments.

If your niche targets first-time investors, then a guide to getting started, like "What I Wish I Knew When Starting" will attract the right customers. Make sure your product targets the correct audience.

A digital product (aka PDF) is a great option for a lead magnet because they are free and easy to distribute. You can set up an email automation to send the PDF directly to their inbox once they have filled in their details. Don't overthink it; a short and sweet resource is better than a 50-page document on market returns. But make it look good; this is the first time your client is seeing your work. Make sure it is something your client will want to read or use.

This strategy has helped me translate my social media growth into an email list full of warm leads. That is the aim of the game.

In my sourcing course, we give you the templates and systems I used so you can use this yourself with no technical ability. You'll get the systems that will generate limitless numbers of free leads (your perfect clients) forever.

But I want to stress that it's not all about quantity; quality will win every time. A friend of mine is a property sourcer, and he has a client list of 12 investors. His entire business is built upon those 12 investors because they are actively looking for properties and have the means to purchase when he finds a good deal. He makes well over 6-figures a year.

12 qualified investors who are hungry for property deals and have the financial means is better than an email list of thousands who are not in a place to buy. Smaller, quality email lists allow you to create healthy, mutually beneficial partnerships because you can get to know your clients a lot better when there are less of them. You

know exactly what they are looking for, and this allows you to give them a more personal experience that will keep them coming back again and again.

Publications and Media

I have been featured in *Vice* and *Business Insider,* along with a number of smaller YouTube channels and local blogs. I have always dreamed of being in *Forbes* (you'll see it one day, I'm determined.) In most of these media appearances, the journalists reached out to me directly after seeing my social media content. It is possible to reach out to journalists and pitch stories to them as well.

Being featured in media brings credibility, especially for well-trusted brands like *Vice* and *Business Insider.* If you get featured in media like this, brag about it everywhere because it improves your street cred and brand authority. Don't just concentrate on the big publications, though; think about where your target audience are. You want to get in front of them as much as possible to position yourself as an expert and connect with your ideal clients. In addition to online and physical publications, consider joining the Facebook Groups where your ideal clients hangout too,

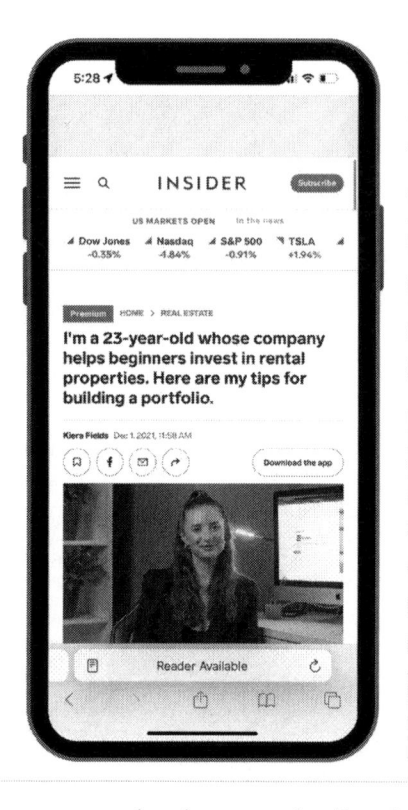

If you're an expert in a local area and sell to locals, then a local newsletter or Facebook group could be an ideal platform for features. They will position you as the local property expert. Offer to write free articles about the property market for them. They get free content, and you get free advertising. Win-win. You can reach out to journalists if you want, but you need to offer them an interesting story. If you get your pitch right, you shouldn't have to pay for the exposure.

Add value to as many people as possible, and you will be rewarded.

Paid Ads

I have not personally used paid ads, but the concept is you are paying to speed up your results. If you don't have a large audience, then you can pay to expand the reach of your content to grow faster. I'm not opposed to the idea of paid ads, but you need to have good content in order to be successful through paid ads. I don't think it is necessary to be successful.

The brilliant thing about paid social media ads is that you only pay to reach the people you want to reach. Years ago, you would've been limited to TV or magazine ads, and your ad would be shown to people who won't work for your niche. The ability to tailor your ad to reach only the most relevant people means that you can reduce your marketing spend. You can select your audience based on location, age, interests, and more. There is an art to getting paid ads right. If you are doing it yourself, there may be a little bit of trial and error before you find the right sales messaging and audience.

Client Acquisition Tools

There are a few tools that will make it easier to find and onboard your ideal clients. They make the process easier and more efficient so you can spend your time elsewhere.

Website

Your website is the cornerstone of your online presence. People can find you organically through search engine results or click on the link on your social media profiles to learn more about what you do and how to work with you. Your website doesn't need to be fancy to get started. It is a place where customers can go to learn more about what you do and how to work with you.

Some people may disagree, but I believe a website is essential for property sourcing. Your website will give you credibility and help your clients feel confident that you are a legit operation. Personally, if I google a company I want to work with, and they don't have an online presence, it's an instant red flag for me.

For me, my website is far more than just my online presence. My background was in IT automation, so I was always looking for ways to use technology to reduce my workload and free up some of my time. One day, I got the (some may say crazy) idea to create something equivalent to Amazon for property. The technology needs some work to get to a place where you can complete the whole process online (though blockchain offers promising possibilities), but I was able to create a store where clients could reserve the property online.

The system was great because it offered a first come, first serve system where clients would fill out the reservation form and pay the reservation fee to claim the deal. As far as I know, nobody else had done this before us. It saves me a lot of time, and I am excited about the possibilities in this space.

When I set it up, I thought no one would buy property directly from the website. In fact, when I got the first sale through the website, I had to call the client and check, but the client said he trusted me, and the property met his needs, so why wouldn't he buy it? My clients trusted me because I had worked to build a relationship with them and prove that I always deliver.

I was in Mallorca for 2 weeks in June, celebrating my birthday, when I got an email telling me my website had been taken down. My heart dropped. That is not an email you want while you're relaxing on a beach. Turns out my website provider had rules against selling porn, guns, and property. Like property belongs in a category with porn and guns! Even though their rule was stupid, I was still without a website. And no website = no sales.

I faced a losing battle trying to get my website back up, so I set up a new site.

Now, I love the creative parts of the job, but I wanted to go back to the beach and relax, so I hired a website designer. I had been ready to level up my website for a while, so I took this as the perfect opportunity to redo my website at the same time.

When you first start, you don't need a fancy website. Having a basic landing page that states your message and how to get in touch is sufficient. That allows you to have an online presence without taking a lot of time and money to set up. As your business grows, you can always update your website if you feel the need.

Your landing page should tell potential clients:

- Who you are
- What you do
- How to contact you

You can set up a website in an afternoon using providers like Wix or WordPress. If you are a bit of a technophobe, you can hire people to set up your website. Fiverr or Upwork are great places to find web designers, graphic designers, or copywriters to help you create your website.

My advice is to keep your website simple and low-cost at the start and then upgrade it once you make more money. It's too easy to get so caught up in making the perfect website that you don't start your business.

Email Marketing System

As your investor list grows, investing in email marketing will be a game-changer. There are so many different email marketing hosts, but I like Mailchimp because it integrates with many of the apps I already use for my business. They offer a free version that is great for when you're starting out, and you can upgrade to paid plans as you need more features or your email list grows. When I first started, keeping costs low was my main priority. Each email marketing provider has different features, so do some research and find the best one for your needs.

Once you have your email list, you want to nurture your leads to keep them warm. To do this, email them regularly to provide valuable, insightful content. Think of your email list as your VIP list. What can you give them that will be insanely useful and have them looking forward to your emails? I recommend weekly emails so you can build a connection with these clients. You can automate the process with your email marketing system, where you write the email in advance and schedule it.

Email Address

Another hack here to look a little more professional is getting a personalised email address. It costs about £5 a month to get an email address with your company name, but it adds a level of professionalism that your clients will respect. Those that ends in @gmail.com or @yahoo.com work in a pinch, but a personalised email address helps you to look like a professional outfit. It is really easy to do, but sometimes it is the simple things that make a difference in business. I see this as taking pride in the smaller details of your business.

Calendly

Calendly was a game-changer in my business. At the start, I used my personal phone number everywhere when setting up my business. It was tied to my Instagram page and my website. This worked perfectly until the first video went viral, and my personal mobile suddenly became a call centre. It would ring day and night with more calls than I could ever answer.

I desperately needed to reclaim my personal mobile number and give clients a better way to contact me. Steve told me about Calendly and recommended I give it a try. So, I set up Calendly. It is a great tool because rather than my phone ringing off the hook, I decide on my available time slots, and potential clients can book in the slot that suits them best. There are no double bookings, and I don't need to hire anyone to manage my calendar or phone. Calendly automatically sends both the client and I a Zoom link so we can log on when it's time for the meeting.

It's a win-win because people can arrange a time for a call that suits them. The call is booked in, and we don't have to play phone tennis because they're expecting my call. Calendly helped me get back control of my schedule.

When I first started using Calendly, I would get on social media at 6 pm on Thursday and advertise that I had 10 available slots. They would book out within half an hour, so I upped it to 20 slots per week. Those would also book out within the hour. Every week our phone slots would sell out. I used to say our phone slots were hotter than tickets to see One Direction.

It was great to see that our phone slots are in such high demand. It shows that people value our expertise. Still, I always felt so bad that I didn't have enough time to meet with everyone who was keen to invest. That is the nature of the business, though; I have to protect my time. I can't spend all week in meetings, at some point, I need to find property deals and sell them too. It has become a little better since I have expanded my team and automated some parts of my business, but more on that later.

CRM

A CRM is a Customer Relationship Manager. Basically, it is a tool that stores all of your customer's information so you can improve the service you offer them.

When I first started KO Estates, everything was on spreadsheets. There were so many spreadsheets and so much information it was frightening. As my business grew, it became much harder to keep track of, and I needed to upgrade to a CRM.

Your CRM will have a profile for each investor where you can keep information about their preferences. This helps me to gather details over our interactions so I can build a clear picture of the type of properties they like. I can also store vendors' and sellers' details in the CRM so I can build better relationships with them too.

There are a number of CRMs out there, so I recommend doing your research to pick the best one for your needs. They do cost, but they are well worth it. When you first start, you can probably get away with a spreadsheet, but as your business grows, invest in a CRM, trust me!

We use Pipedrive now but were previously on another system. My advice following this migration process is to keep your database accurate and consistent throughout. You are only as good as your data, and when you start growing, your database can get very messy very quickly. My biggest tip would be to do it right from day 1 and update your database as you go, so the information is always up to date.

Go and Do It

You need to build an investor list, so you have someone to sell the deals to. Start by promoting your business in these places.

- Social media – Most of my investors find me because I post about what I do on social media. I show the results I get for my clients and the type of properties I source so I attract the right types of investors.

Once you niche down, it is easy to create content that attracts the right kind of people. Pick a social media platform and set up an account. Start posting regularly so you can build a following.

- Publications and media – I have been lucky enough to be featured in *Vice* and *Business Insider*. This adds credibility to my business and gets me and my business in front of a new audience. Reach out to them and offer to write articles that share your expertise about the area or property type you sell.
- Email list – Not everyone who follows you on social media will be an investor. Build an email list full of warm leads who are ready to invest or almost ready to invest.

A key factor to your success will be how well you understand your ideal investors. When you understand their pain points, and why they want to invest, you can tailor your service to cater to their needs. You can also focus your efforts where they hang out online.

Building a Relationship with Investors

Getting investors is important, but you want to make the most of all your hard work by keeping your investors. Nurturing your database is crucial to keeping your leads warm and keeping your business front of mind. The key is continuing to build a relationship.

Client Journey

Property is a long-term game, so the client journey is more important here than in any other industry. The type of money involved in property means that your clients won't make an impulse buy. Paying attention to the client journey helps you to nurture your clients and keep them long-term. If your client is ready to buy, you want to keep them warm until you find the right deal. If they are not ready to buy yet, you can actively help them to get in a position to buy.

Everyone's client journey looks different. This is the general path most of our clients follow:

1. Follow us on social media
2. Download a freebie and sign up for our email list
3. Nurtured via email / social channel
4. Phone call to discuss their needs
5. Viewing (optional)
6. Sold

This section is all about steps 3 and 4. We are keeping our investor list warm, keeping our services front of mind, and using this time to build credibility and trust. This is an important step because the investor needs to be confident in our abilities before we present the deal. That way, they don't need to be "sold" to, they know what you do and how you do it, and they're keen to work with you.

Nurturing Clients via Email or Social Channels - KNOW LIKE TRUST

Know, like, and trust is important because you are asking clients to invest a large amount of money. People generally do business with people they know, like, and trust.

Think of where you get your coffee. There are probably a couple of places you could get coffee, but you go to the same place every time you want coffee. This is because you know the brand, you like the coffee they serve, and you trust that you will always receive good coffee and service. I go to Starbucks because I know the brand; it is instantly recognisable anywhere I am. I like the coffee and atmosphere, and I trust that I have the same experience no matter where I am in the world.

If you want to become a person of influence or the go-to person for property investment, you need to:

- Be known for providing high-quality products and services
- Be approachable and likeable
- Be trustworthy

Here's how you achieve each of those things.

Know

You need to let people get to know you. This is why I recommend using your face on social media. You need to show up and constantly remind them who you are so you can strengthen their association with your personal brand.

This means showing up on social media regularly (daily if you need to) or sending them emails to open a direct line of communication with them. Remind them what you do and let them know that you are still in business. Keep your message clear and consistent for maximum results.

You've probably heard this a thousand times, but people buy from people they know. So, the trick is to be open and honest. People appreciate it when people are real and true on social media. Show the downs just as much as the ups, and you will stand out on Instagram. Instagram can feel like a highlight reel a lot of the time, so people will connect with you if they see that you face some of the same struggles they do.

At every touchpoint, make sure it is clear what you do and what service you provide. This will help you become known as the expert in the game.

Like

Your message will receive greater reach if people like you. Being likeable and approachable will make it easier to attract the clients you want to work with.

People may find likeability in your:

- Morals
- Values
- Personality
- How you conduct business
- Results
- Knowledge
- How you make them feel

Every person is likeable; you wouldn't have friends otherwise. The key is letting that likeability come across online.

So how do you allow your likeability to translate? Let people get to know you. People feel instantly more connected to people they feel like they know or people who are vulnerable with them. So let people get to know you as a person.

Don't worry about pleasing everyone who comes across your social media. Just show up as your authentic self and show that you really care for your clients. The right people will be attracted to what you are doing.

Trust

Trust is key to doing business with someone. Would you give someone you trust money? No! So why would someone part with a huge sum of money if they don't trust you?

You have to build trust as you are building a relationship with your clients. Start from the very first touchpoint. Build trust in your first call with the client so that when the right deal comes along, they are already on board with what you do.

Building trust is easier than you think. It is all about delivering on what you have promised. If you said you would do something, do it. This can be as simple as calling when you said you would or sending an email you said you would send. Follow through on your promises, and your clients will see you as trustworthy. The more honest and transparent you are, the more you will build trust.

You can also build trust through your previous work. We always share success stories, reviews, and feedback. Future clients can see that we have gotten past clients amazing results. Your clients can see that other clients enjoyed working with you. **Make sure to shout about every win, build your credibility, show people what you do.**

Trust is everything in the property sourcing game. There is a lot of money involved, so there needs to be trust. The minute a client doesn't trust you, the deal is gone. There is no way they are spending hundreds of thousands on a property you recommend.

You are a one-person brand right now, but that is an advantage. It is much easier to build a personal brand than it is a corporate brand. People buy from people, after all. Your followers are more likely to feel connected to you as an individual than they are a big, faceless organisation. So, use it to your advantage. Show up for your clients and add value instead of always trying to sell. Let them get to know, like, and trust you so they can contemplate buying from you.

Phone call

A phone call is the next active step in a client's journey, putting a voice/face to your digital interactions so far. If you are at this stage, you know clients are keen and interested. This step can also be time-consuming, so it's important you are getting the most out of your time with your client. Make sure you get all the information you need, and they get the best experience.

Investors are not all the same, even when you niche down. Each of your clients will be different in terms of their wants, needs, and how they think. You cannot create a one-size-fits-all approach, especially not when your clients are choosing to spend a considerable amount of money with you. Understand each investor and their pain points so you can become the solution to their problem.

When I first started out, I wasn't using this phone call wisely. I would get caught chatting away to a client only to realise when I hung up that I didn't have any of the information I needed to help the client. There were also times when I spent hours searching for a property for a client, only to completely miss the brief. This situations were disappointing because I had wasted valuable time because I hadn't asked the right questions or clarified information that I didn't understand. I can't afford to waste that time, so now I follow the MAN framework with every client. This helps me to really understand what it is they want. MAN stands for Motivation, Ability, and Needs.

Motivation

What is their why? By that, I mean, why are they investing in property? Everyone has different priorities; your investor could be investing in property for:

- Security
- Passive income
- Retirement fund
- To Quit their job

All of these reasons are valid, and each reason comes with a different set of priorities. Someone who is investing in property for passive income will prioritise cash flow. Someone investing in property for security will want diversification. Someone investing in property for retirement will prioritise long-term gains.

Ability

I like to look at ability in terms of **financial ability** and **time ability.**

Financial Ability

You could present the best deal in the world, but if your investor does not have the financial ability, then they cannot buy the deal.

It is important to understand what stage your investor is at. They may be getting to know you in order to invest in the future rather than looking to invest right now. You can find their ability by asking a few probing questions like, "Tell me where you are in your property journey?" That should give you an indication of when they are ready to go.

Ask how much working capital they have. You need to know:

- What they can afford
- How much they are willing to invest
- How they are financing the purchase

Understanding their total budget, including the budget if the property needs work, will help you to filter deals for them. It may feel nosy to ask these questions, but you don't want to waste their time (or yours) by showing them unsuitable deals.

Time Ability

Just because a client is not ready to buy a deal right now does not mean they are not a great client. In the property sourcing game, you need to take a long-term approach to working with clients. Life gets in the way a lot, so even the clients that are ready right now are not guaranteed to buy.

Sure, you may want to sell deals right now, but having a pipeline of customers who will get in touch within 6-12 months is a great thing. You are building a list of future customers.

If your clients are not ready right now, then make a good impression by talking them through the next steps. For example, if your client is currently saving for their deposit, recommend that they speak to a mortgage broker so they can understand their budget. You could also suggest they speak to an accountant to set up a business account so they can purchase their property.

By giving them advice rather than writing them off, they will think of you when they are ready to buy a deal.

I suggest partnering and working with professionals like accountants, solicitors, and mortgage brokers. Your clients will find value in receiving a list of hand-selected professionals from you. It creates a win-win-win.

- Your clients get a list of recommended local service providers
- Your partners get referrals
- You ensure your clients work with service providers who are good at what they do (read: they won't slow down the process.)

Needs

Take the time to understand the needs of your investors. What is on their list of musts, and what is on their list of wants?

Your client may prefer a freehold property over a leasehold or an apartment over a house, for example.

Always ask why so you can understand the reason behind these wants. They may have these needs because of a lack of education. For example, I often hear investors who are adamant they will not accept a leasehold property. In London, there are leasehold scandals where leaseholders for apartment buildings keep raising the rate. In the North, where I specialise, this isn't the case. The leasehold on my own place is £12 per year. So, find out why they have their needs because sometimes you can educate them and help them not miss out on otherwise great deals. Education is a key part of the sales process.

Gather the information about motivation, ability, and needs on the first call with the client. Store the information in a database so you can refer to it in the future. You may not have a deal that suits their needs right now, that's ok. When new deals come up, you can view your database to find a buyer ready to go. It becomes more like matchmaking.

You will speak to some clients who are generally really keen to get started in property investing but are not in a position to buy just yet.

This may seem frustrating because you just wasted your time when you could have been finding more deals or talking to people who are ready to buy. That is the wrong attitude to have. If you thank them for their time and write them off, then you will never hear from this client again, not even when they are ready to buy.

Instead, think long-term. Often if someone is not ready to buy, they just need a few pieces of the puzzle to fall into place. Most of our clients are first-time buyers and feel overwhelmed by the process and aren't quite sure where to start. If we help them to get ready to buy, then we are the first person they think of when they're ready to start looking at deals. This differentiates us from our competition because not many property sourcers take the time to do this.

Doing this takes very little time. We have a PDF that we can send out that talks them through the steps to preparing to buy. It provides a list of companies and services we recommend and explains each step of the process.

Most of the time, they just need help setting up a business to purchase their investment property. So, we recommend an accountant and explain what they need to do. When we recommend clients to an affiliated accountant, they often tell us when the client is ready to go. Sometimes, they just need to speak to a mortgage advisor to find out how much they can borrow and how to secure funding.

These are very easy things to do, but they help the client immensely, so they think of you favourably. You will gain a client in the long-term because you helped them when other companies didn't want to speak until they were ready to buy.

Clients who ring to discuss property investment are keen to invest, but they can easily give up when they reach the first hurdle. The buying process can seem overwhelming to first-time buyers. By giving them the information they need, we help them keep their momentum up. They are grateful for our help and are keen to work with us once they are in a position to buy. They also rave about us to their friends and family.

Whilst we are building a list of investors and buyers, we need to make sure that we know what it is exactly what they want. We are building a profile for them so we want to get as much information as possible from the client on these areas because it will save them and us a huge amount of time and allow us to build an unlimited pipeline of clients if we get it right. It's also going to become the foundation of our sales process, which comes next.

Go and Do It

Now that you have your investors, the trick is to keep them around. You spent a lot of time and potentially money getting the investor on your client list, so building a long-term relationship maximises the value of the investor. They may buy multiple properties over the course of a few years.

Keep your investors around by continuing to build a relationship with them. They need to know, like, and trust you in order to buy property from you. The best way to do this is to add value. Tailor your service to give them exactly what they want and need. Listen to their recommendations and look for ways you can continue to improve. This is how to fill your client list with raving fans.

Start by writing down all of your client pain points, from small niggling annoyances through to massive issues. Look for ways you can reduce the impact of these pain points or eliminate them completely. Could you create a resource that, after the initial work, can address a pain point for all future clients? Are there pain points you can address to provide a better experience for your clients?

The Sales Process

Okay, so you have a deal, and you have a growing list of investors. Now what?

Now, you need to be a matchmaker. It is time to match your deal with an investor. My first point of call is the investor database, where I have the specifics of what everyone is looking for. Start by talking to people who have indicated that they are looking for something that matches your deal based on the location and investment type. If they have asked for a specific feature that is present in the deal, then even better, it should be an easy win.

By going to investors in your database who match the deal before sharing it on social media, you strengthen the relationship. It shows that your client list will always be prioritised, and therefore, it is a worthwhile list to be on. Your client list feels like they are part of an exclusive list, and you get to say, "I saw this property and thought of you." FOMO is a fantastic way to grow your email list.

How We Created Our Sales Process

In August 2021, I secured a 60-house portfolio. This was a game-changer for my business. It translated to more deals and more sourcing fees.

Most of the properties in the portfolio were located in Blackpool, and my dad lived in the area, so I brought my dad on board to help me sell them. We spent a lot of time working out our strategy. I had sold a few deals, but I was still in the trial-and-error phase. With this deal, I wanted to create a strategy. I knew that this deal would lead to my success if I handled it right.

My dad and I agreed that pricing the deal correctly was vital. A 5% yield may not attract much interest, but a 7% yield would be very attractive. We had received a marketing mail out from Virgin Money promoting a new easy-access ISA as an amazing deal offering a 0.3% interest rate. This was an amazing deal in terms of bank interest rates. It was far above what any other bank offered. So, we realised that if we wanted our deals to be attractive, we needed to completely surpass what was on the market. At 7%, we were offering a yield 21 times higher than an ISA. The ISA would give a return of £75 per year, and our properties, on average, were offering £6240 per year for a £25,000 deposit.

A 7% yield was the sweet spot for us because it offered enough of a return to offset any of the reasons buyers would be nervous about investing in real estate. Again, I worked with a lot of first-time buyers. Real estate investment opportunities offer monthly cash flow, so a 7% yield just makes the deal a no-brainer. This is something that is key in business; you need to offer your clients something so good that they feel silly saying no to it.

The seller was on board with sales prices that created the 7% yield; why wouldn't he be? He was selling his property portfolio without having to pay anything. Usually, he would have to pay estate agent fees.

All 60 properties were tenanted. When we spoke to estate agents, they said that tenanted properties were not attractive to buyers. According to them, buyers like to start fresh. This worried us for a little bit, but we decided to ask our audience. I put a poll up on my Instagram asking if property investors prefer to buy a property empty or with tenants in place. The results said the opposite of what estate agents told us. Over 90% of people who responded said they wanted to buy a property with tenants in place. It made sense; it was one less thing for them to do.

Most of our audience was between 25 and 40 years of age, and most importantly, they lived south of Birmingham. We realised that the fact that our client pool lived far away gave us an opportunity. We could package the deal in a way that made it more attractive. The poll showed us that our clients valued deals that required little work on their part. It made sense to create a package that reduced the clients' workload even more.

We thought about what services the client would need to start earning rental income quickly. They would need a:

- Mortgage broker
- Solicitor
- Letting agent

My clients didn't live locally, so I saw a chance for me to add more value by recommending those professionals to my clients. This would save them a lot of time researching and meeting with professionals. We had created an offer that our clients wanted. It basically sold itself. We simply presented our clients with 2 facts:

1. Putting £25k savings into a bank account would earn you £75 a year in interest. Putting £25k savings into a house will give you

£6240 per year in rent, and there is the potential for capital appreciation in the future too.

2. We had just sold a house in Blackpool for £74k. The client paid a £23k cash deposit and borrowed £51k on an interest-only mortgage. The interest payments were £101 per month, and the tenant paid £563 per month in rent.

The value was very clear from those two facts. Some clients even paid without seeing the property. They were happy with our comprehensive reports and the pictures online.

I like to shout about every sale we make. I share it on social media, on my website, and everywhere I can. Sharing the results of your business builds trust. It proves that you complete sales. I post a dance with the figures of each sale. It also provides easy, popular content. People love seeing behind the scenes content.

If the deal is completed quickly, even better. Your service becomes more desirable. Next time you share a deal, people will know they need to act quickly if they want to buy your deal. Get testimonials from customers after each sale to build your credibility. Share them on social media and on your website as social proof. Rinse and repeat this process. Not only did we use this process to sell all 60 of these houses, but it became the backbone of the process we use in KO Estates today. There are 5 steps to the KO Estates Sales Process:

1. Know the Product
2. Present the Deal
3. Chat with Qualified Buyers
4. Reservation
5. MOS

Know the Product

Knowing your product inside and out is crucial to long-term property sourcing success. I would never sell a property I haven't seen, and I will never sell a property that I didn't believe in.

Before I take a property on, I do a full due diligence, so I feel confident selling it to my clients. This includes:

- The property's story (history, why it's being sold, interesting facts, etc.)
- Where the property is located (demographics, employment rates, amenities, etc.)
- The numbers of the deal
- What work is required
- Deal packaging (tenants, legal, etc.)

These details help me to bring the property to life when I am talking to clients. More importantly, these are the details your clients will want to know. You need to know them so you can answer their questions confidently.

We sell properties with tenants in place, so we get to know the tenants a little bit. We can tell our clients:

- Tenants' names
- Tenants' jobs
- Rent payment history

The more details you know about the property, tenants, and the area, the better equipped you are to sell the deal to your clients. Paint a picture of the investment opportunity. When you can tell them why the tenant demand is high and why tenants would want to live in the property, the opportunity becomes more real and more attractive to your clients.

At KO Estates, we prepare for every possible question our client may have about the property. In some cases, we know more about the property than the seller!

Present the Deal

Your deal is your offer. Take some time on the presentation. Good presentation will show you are a professional outfit and strengthen the trust of your investors.

How much information your deal provides will depend on where you found the deal. If you found the deal on a property portal, like Rightmove, then you shouldn't give too much information. The more information you give on Rightmove deals, the easier it will be for your clients to find the deal for themselves and cut you out of the deal. They can save themselves your sourcing fee and contact the seller and their agent through Rightmove. So, it is best to hold back on some of the details until you have a contract in place to protect you.

Once they have signed the contract, you can share the property details with them without worrying that they will cut you out of the deal. The signed document means they commit to buying the property through you.

The ideal situation is when a vendor gives you exclusive access to an off-market property. You can be extremely open and honest with your investors and give them the details they need to perform due diligence. You don't even need to get them to sign a contract because you have an agreement with the vendor that stops them from cutting you out.

When you have this type of agreement, you can be really creative with your marketing. There is no need to worry about being cut out of the deal, so you can promote the deal on social media and get it in front of more people.

Your deal needs to include the following details. These are the things your investors need to know:

- Location – Include information about the demographics of the area, rental demand, and what there is to do locally.
- Numbers – Include the breakdown of the purchase price, expected rental income, ground rent, management fees, construction fees (if it needs renovations), yield, and investment stacks.
- Management – Include a recommendation for a management company. Provide information about how much they charge.
- Capital appreciation – Provide the history of the area's property market.
- Comparables – Share the sale price for similar properties in the area that were recently sold. This will prove that it is a good deal.

Clarity is everything when you present these details. Don't overcomplicate things, just include the necessary details in an easy-to-read format. If you overwhelm or confuse your clients, they are more likely to say no, so keep things simple and easy to understand.

Here is an example of one of my deals in a template I use time and time again

www.property-sourcing-secrets.com/example-deal

If it is an off-market exclusive deal, mention it. This makes the deal more desirable – people want what they can't have. An exclusive deal means that they have access to something that others can't get. That makes them feel special, and you prove that being on your email list is worthwhile.

Send your deal out to your investor list and make a few calls to notify particular investors if previous conversations make you believe the property would work particularly well for them. If it is an exclusive deal, share it on social media.

Chat With Qualified Buyers

When you send out your great deal via social media and email lists, you will receive a lot of interest. The trick is to narrow that interest down so you can focus on the qualified buyers. Your time is precious, and you need to protect it at all costs. You don't have time to show properties to people who are not in a position to buy, and your vendor will not appreciate the disruption of unnecessary viewings. Identify the following things in your initial conversation:

- Do they have the funding available?
- If the right property came up tomorrow, would they be ready to go?

You may also get interest from people who are interested in property investment but not in a position to buy. Like I said, that is okay; they are potential future clients. I like to nurture these clients and build a relationship because then they come to me when they are ready.

Once you've determined that a client is ready to buy, it's time to uncover what they're looking for. Talk to them about why they are investing in property, and why they are interested in this property. The property may not be right for their needs, and they will appreciate you taking the time to understand what they are looking for rather than shoehorning them into a sale. You can add them to your database and keep your eye out for a deal that is better suited to their needs.

Once you have your list narrowed down to suitable buyers and ready-to buy buyers, further qualify by requesting proof of funds.

Proof of Funds

Proof of funds is CRUCIAL. Never move forward with a deal until you have proof of funds.

Again, this is a lesson I learned the hard way. I have been disappointed by clients when I sold a deal only to find out that the client was struggling to get a mortgage. When a client pulls out, you're back to square one. It wastes so much time, so you want to avoid that by covering your bases. Seeing proof of funds will do this. Affordability checks are important to make sure you are happy to move forward with the client. This is as important as whether the client is happy to move forward with the deal.

This is a lot more difficult for mortgage buyers because, at the end of the day, it is all down to the lender. But you can ask the client to show you the decision in principle. This is a certificate the lender gives a prospective buyer to confirm the amount they are happy to lend. It's not a guarantee, but it provides more certainty than you would otherwise have. It tells you that the client has started the mortgage process and how much money they have been offered.

I ask to see up-to-date proof of funds before I will let anyone secure a deal. For cash buyers, screenshots of their bank account with the money in it will suffice. For mortgage buyers, we need to see proof of funds for the deposit and the mortgage in principle certificate. It can be a difficult discussion to have; nobody likes to talk money, least of all Brits. The good news is, securing proof of funds has become standard practice with estate agents since the pandemic, so it's not unexpected. It will help you to identify if your client is actually in a place to buy.

Cash Buyers vs Mortgages

Cash buyers make for a much smoother process than a buyer with a mortgage. There are fewer parties involved, so you can influence the efficiency of the process.

When you work with a mortgage buyer, the mortgage company needs to evaluate the quality of the sale. They will organise surveyors and valuations. You are also reliant on the mortgage offer, and it can sometimes fall through. For example, following Grenfell mortgage companies are requiring testing of apartment buildings to ensure the cladding meets new codes. This is the case even when an apartment building does not have cladding. Currently, specialists have waiting lists for appointments, so this can take months to sign off.

Even though cash buyers are easier to work with, they are quite rare. Most buyers understandably opt to leverage good debt to maximise their budget. I'm not including this section to put you off ever working with mortgage buyers. I just think it is important information to allow you to adjust your estimated timeline. This is also another great argument for recommending mortgage providers to your clients. You can recommend mortgage companies that are efficient and don't block sales for seemingly arbitrary reasons. This will make your life much easier because nine times out of ten, your client will be working with a preferred partner.

Reservation

Make it official before you go any further. Having a reservation process in place protects both you and the seller from flaky buyers. It reduces the likelihood of buyers backing out because they have skin in the game. If the buyer does back out, then there are clear expectations and stipulations in place.

Reservation Form

Always get a reservation form. Another lesson I learned the hard way. Please learn from my mistakes.

At KO Estates, we speak with our investors, often multiple times. This builds a relationship based on trust that goes both ways. We trust our clients and enjoy working with them. But sometimes we trust our clients too much.

In this situation, we got caught out big time. We were working with a client to purchase their 2nd property with us. They were a long-term client with plans to build an investment portfolio with us. They wanted to complete some work on the property before they purchased it. We agreed to complete the work before they bought the property.

Now, if we had a reservation agreement, everything would have been fine, but naively, we didn't. We went ahead with the work because we had verbal agreements, and we trusted the client. I do believe that the client had every intention of buying the property. I want to be clear that they didn't mean any harm. Unfortunately, between talking to the client and completing the work, the client's financial situation changed, and they pulled out of the purchase. This happens all the time in property purchases. The only thing is we were on the hook for the cost of renovations.

I was sourcing property deals to make money, and I ended up losing money. It was an expensive lesson, but it meant I did not make that mistake again. In hindsight, it seems like such a stupid mistake. I was still new to running a business, and it was really easy to blur the lines between clients and friends.

The thing is, buying property is not a quick process. It can take months to get from purchase agreement to completion. And in that time, sometimes situations change. My process includes a 7-day cooling-off period for my clients. After that, the sourcing fee is non-refundable. I recommend you implement this policy and make it a term of your signed reservation form. Point it out to your clients before they sign so they are aware of it. Hopefully, you don't have to rely on it, but if you do, then you have it in writing.

Another essential term for your reservation agreement is the timeframe. I have had clients who have purchased the deal and then dragged their feet through progression due to a lack of funds. Progression usually takes less than 3 months, but they stretched it out to 6 months.

If the deal takes too long to complete, you will sour your relationship with the vendor. They are working with you because you promised to find them a buyer quickly. The longer it takes for the property to complete, the longer their life is on hold. Time is money for you, for your clients, and for the property vendor. There will often be industry delays that are outside of your control. Surveys could cause delays; it was a real nightmare during Covid. A time-frame clause will protect you and your vendor if your client drags their feet. Your time-frame clause could state something like if the client takes longer than 3 months to complete, you have the right to remarket the property and not return the fees.

Your reservation form protects you, the vendor, and the client. Everyone knows what is expected of them. Get a signed reservation form, sourcing fee, and reservation fee before you move forward with the deal.

Sourcing Fee / Reservation Deposit

A sourcing fee is a fee your client pays you for finding them the deal. This is how your property sourcing business makes money. You can structure this however it makes sense for your business. I charge my sourcing fee 50% upfront and 50% on completion. It is possible to charge the entirety of your sourcing fee up front, but I found that my method builds trust with clients. They trust you to help you right up until completion because you lose half your fee if the deal falls through.

So, when the client reserves the deal, they pay 50% of the sourcing fee and a reservation deposit while you complete the sales process. This proves that the client is serious, and they are more likely to go through to completion because they have skin in the game. The upfront payment of a non-refundable sourcing fee protects your time. The non-refundable reservation deposit compensates the vendor for the inconvenience of the sale taking longer because you have to find another buyer.

Some people who are new to the property investing world don't understand sourcing fees. The concept is foreign to them because buyers don't pay fees to the estate agents. Unfortunately, some people are not happy to pay the sourcing fee, so prepare to be challenged. A sourcing fee is easily justified by the time and effort you put into finding the deal. Most of your clients will understand that you provide value by finding deals they would otherwise not be able to find.

On smaller deals, I charge a £2,000 sourcing fee but do whatever works best for you. The sourcing fee could be anything up to 5% of the price of the property to meet industry standards. I like to tailor my sourcing fee depending on the size of the deal and the amount of value I added.

The reservation deposit should be at least £1,000, but the size of the deposit should reflect the size of the deal. The purpose of the reservation deposit is to make sure your client is invested enough in the deal that they won't pull out. It protects the time and effort you and the vendor have put in.

Memorandum of Sale

Once you have agreed to the sale and secured the sourcing fee and reservation fee, you need to kick-start the purchase process. Get moving right away because it can be a lengthy process to completion. The way to start the purchase process is to create a MOS.

An MOS is a Memorandum of Sale. It is a document that states all of the purchase deals. All of the parties involved get a copy of the MOS, and it instructs the soliciting process.

It has to contain the following information:

- Full property address
- Agreed price
- Purchaser's name
- Details for the purchaser's solicitor
- Vendor's name
- Details for the vendor's solicitor
- Agent's name (you)
- Agent's contact details (your contact details)
- Outstanding sourcing fee payment (if applicable)

Make sure the outstanding sourcing fee payment is clear on the MOS if you need to be paid on completion. This ensures your payment is a term of the sale. Your payment will come through the solicitor upon completion, so you don't have to chase the client for payment. If the remaining sourcing fee is not paid, then the sale cannot legally proceed.

How to Structure Your Fees

The success of your business all starts here. How you structure your fees will influence the profit you make from the work you do and also your relationship with your clients.

Talking about money is definitely not easy, so I am here to tell you that you deserve to be paid. You offer a valuable service to your clients, and you work damn hard. Many people, unfortunately, see property sourcing as a really low-effort business. The misconception is that we're finding deals off Zoopla and sending them to people in exchange for money. Property sourcing is a lot of work, and we are a partner to our clients for the entire process.

There are a number of ways you can structure your fees, and I have used all of these at some point for KO Estates. Generally, I use a sourcing fee, but I tailor my fee to the circumstances of the deal.

Sourcing Fee

The most common way property sourcers make money is by charging a sourcing fee. This is the most transparent way to do things. The client knows exactly how much they are paying you for bringing them this deal.

Most clients have no problem paying a sourcing fee, especially if they are investors who have done it all before. They see the value you provide and know that you will earn your fee.

Unfortunately, some clients don't like the idea of paying a sourcing fee or will be offended by the size of your sourcing fee. The best way to handle these disagreements is to justify your value and remind them that they would not have found this deal without your help. Unfortunately, in some cases, the deal will break down over the sourcing fee. It is best to just let those clients go because they don't value what you do. Never reduce or eliminate your sourcing fee; you will just end up resenting the client.

Back-to-Back Agreements

This is a more discreet way of handling your fees and is often used for high-value deals. The solicitor structures the contracts in a way so both parties only see the price that is relevant to them.

The vendor only sees the agreed-upon sale price, and the buyer only sees the price they have agreed to pay. Neither sees the price the other is getting and therefore do not know what you are earning. For example, the vendor will sell their property to you for £90,000. You charge a sourcing fee of £15,000. So, the purchaser will see the price as £105,000.

This is fine as long as both parties are getting a good deal.

Not every solicitor will structure a deal this way, so use a solicitor who has done this before. It is a little more complex, so the solicitor will charge more for this service.

We have never used this method at KO Estates, and I advise you only do it if you really need to. My motto is honesty is the best policy. I worry that I would slip and tell one of the parties the wrong price. It can be tricky, so only use it if you have a good reason.

Charging the Vendor

Property sourcers usually work for the buyer, but in some cases, you are really helping the vendor to sell. They are saving money on estate agent's fees, so you could charge them a fee for finding them a buyer quickly and saving them money.

Overage Agreement

This is basically putting your charge on top. This is similar to back-to-back agreements, but the vendor knows how much you are making. The client still doesn't know how much you are charging in this scenario.

Basically, the vendor tells you how much they want to make on the sale and are happy for you to charge whatever fee you want on top. They receive a contract with the price the buyer is paying, so they know how much you sell their property for.

The buyer receives the sale price as a total; your fee is not broken down in the price. You get paid on completion.

Create Raving Fans Who Come Back for More

Throughout the entire sales process, our approach is not just to gain clients but to gain raving fans who come back to us again and again. Raving fans are obsessed with your business. They share your social media posts, recommend you to their friends and co-workers, and always contact you when they need to buy property. They love your business and service so much that they would never consider contacting another property sourcer.

Your raving fans will always talk about your business when they hear someone talking about property investment (and sometimes even when it doesn't come up in conversation.) This is the best advertising you can dream of. It is completely free, and they are speaking to people who trust their opinion. Their passion is infectious, and even complete strangers will get on board after hearing their rave reviews.

Raving fans will stick with you through thick and thin. They are the best clients to work with, and you need to show your appreciation.

How to Get Raving Fans

Raving fans connect to your business on a deeper level. Here are some of the things that help you to create this type of engagement.

Values

Your raving fans share the same values as your business. When your customers see your brand online, they must know what you stand for. Raving fans will believe in your values just as strongly as you do.

Your values will set you apart from others in your industry. They help to build trust with your audience because clients can predict how you may act in different situations based on your values. In order to build trust and connection through your values, you need to live and breathe them every day, in every interaction. Build your values into everything you do as a business.

Know Your Audience

Once you have identified your ideal clients, you need to know everything you can about them.

Create a customer avatar for your dream clients and fill it with information about their motivations and what they need from a property. Tailor your content, processes, and communication to this avatar.

Start by writing down your ideal client's:

- Age range
- Gender
- Location
- Budget
- Profession
- Availability during the day
- Interests and Hobbies – What do they read, and what websites do they frequent?
- Where they hang out – Join groups they are a part of so you can understand them (both online and in-person groups)
- The problems they face – Understand their pain points so you can create a service that solves them.
- What they appreciate – Find out what will make working with you a little more pleasurable. Pleasure points are just as important as pain points.

Connect the Dots

Show your customers how you will take them from where they are now to where they want to be. Get them excited about the plan you have for them and show them what the next steps are.

The easier it is for your clients to understand what you do and how you do it, the more likely they are to work with you. The easier and more convenient you make it, the lower the barrier to entry. You will create a reputation for being an innovative leader just by making things more convenient for your customers.

Customer Service

Customer service costs nothing, but this is something that came up a lot in our feedback as to why our clients love working with us. This is an area that we put a lot of effort into from the very start, and I believe it's a big reason for our success. Some of the things we do are answering customer enquiries whenever our clients need us, making things as simple as possible, and always trying to go above and beyond. We made our clients feel looked after, and it gained their trust. The best part is customer service doesn't cost you anything but your time.

Deliver More Than You Promised

Overdeliver on your service. Give your customers more value than they expected, and you will leave an excellent impression. When you overpromise and under-deliver, people feel cheated and disappointed. They had an expectation in their heads when they paid you, and they feel like they didn't get their money's worth. They might even go as far as to discourage people from working with you.

When you exceed their expectations, they will remember you forever and recommend you to the people they know. Think about how you can go one step further to make the experience more enjoyable or add more value to the clients. We try to always look for ways we can improve our clients' experience.

Think about when you go on holiday. I love travelling and always enjoy going on holiday. I spend a lot of time researching to ensure I have an enjoyable time away. Some of the hotels I have visited have a little welcome gift. It is usually something small like a complimentary drink at check-in or some chocolates or snacks in the room. These little extra touches make for a nicer experience. I didn't expect them, but they were nice to have. Think about what you can do to add a nice extra touch for your customers.

In our business, many of our clients are not local to the area, but just like everyone else, they want to do a viewing before they purchase the deal. Some of our clients travel up to 4 hours. If they worked with an estate agent, they would drive 4 hours for a 10-minute viewing and then drive 4 hours back home. We know that when we have driven a long distance to a viewing, it seems a waste if the viewing is just 10 minutes.

What we do is greet them with a coffee so they can refresh after a long drive and show them the local area as well as the property or properties they came to view. We take the time to walk them through why we picked the investment for them and point out things they should look through on a viewing. If the client is a first-time buyer, we add value by walking them through the whole buying process, so they feel confident. Little things like this can make a big difference to your clients.

Understand your audience, understand their problems, and ask yourself what you can do to enhance their experience. In our case, our client's problem is that they have been in a car for 4 hours. They haven't eaten or freshened up for that time. By identifying that, we were able to put ourselves in their shoes to think of what we would need after a long drive. Coffee would be number one on my list. I would also want to maximise the day so I didn't have to come back, and I felt the drive was worth it.

Reward Best Customers

Reward your best clients for their loyalty and thank them for coming back. When you make your clients feel special, they will keep returning. Referral schemes are a great example of this; your client gets a discount each time they recommend a friend.

You can offer discounts if you wish, but Christmas or birthday gifts are a nice touch too. They make people feel special and like you were thinking of them. People will forget the details of dealing with you as time goes by, but they will never forget the way you made them feel. So, make them feel special.

Always Listen

Always ask for feedback so you can understand your audience. Send out surveys and look for ways to keep improving. At KO Estates, feedback is one of our most important metrics for success. It allows us to keep our customers happy.

We implement changes in response to our feedback. I believe this makes our customers feel empowered to give feedback because they know we really listen to it. They can see their feedback in action.

Run polls on social media, ask them to email you with questions, or ask them for ideas. My recommendation is to ask your audience using every channel you have. That way, you can serve your clients better at every stage of the customer journey.

Transparency

The best way to build trust in an industry that seems untrustworthy is to be transparent. If you show up with honesty and are clear about the process, and manage your client's expectations, you will gain trust and respect.

Nothing can be hidden with property. Your client can do a Google search and find the property history from Zoopla, so you will be caught out if you are not honest and transparent. Transparency from the very start is key to building quality relationships with your clients.

Community

Building a community within your business is a great way to make people feel like they are part of something bigger. It feels like a club where you are surrounded by like-minded people. Your clients can meet people who are also doing what they are doing or want to do.

Create a community where your clients feel safe and their success is celebrated. Your clients can help each other and have group chats where they share their struggles and successes. You can create a community using Facebook Groups or by starting a group chat. It is free and easy to start but will create raving fans.

Add Value

Do more than your competition. This all boils down to knowing everything you can about your audience. What are their problems, what do their days look like, and what do they want to achieve?

I'll be the first to admit that selling a 2 up 2 down in Blackpool is not very glamorous. There are no stunning views or beautiful architectural features to sell the property for us. But I had a secret weapon.

I know that our clients are busy professionals. They have money but very little time. They don't live in the area, so they value everything being as easy as possible. Our clients want an expert when it comes to property. They want someone who can make the process quick and easy.

So, we packaged the property in a way that would meet the goals of the audience.

- Tenant in place - We put a tenant in place so they could start earning money from the get-go. They can see the tenant's payment track record, so they don't have to worry about missed payments.
- Management agency - We put a management agency in place, so the client didn't have to spend time finding someone. The management agency had local contacts, so they could secure people to do repairs quickly without bothering the client.
- Mortgage advice – We partnered with a mortgage expert so our clients could organise a mortgage quickly.
- Renovated and Ready – We often renovate the properties so they are ready to go when the client gets the keys. Our out-of-town clients don't have the contacts to arrange work or the time or ability to oversee progress. This was a way we could add more value by making everything as easy as

possible and removing any possible barrier to the sale. This covers everything from a little touch-up to full renovations depending on what the property needs. The client doesn't have to do a single thing. Our goal is to remove any resistance in the process.

Basically, we built a dream team so our clients had all of the services they needed from start to finish. They could start earning money with very little work on their part. By packaging each of our properties as a ready-to-go deal, we addressed our clients' pain points. They didn't have time to research everything and mess around with the finer details, so we sorted those things for them.

By packaging our deals in a way that solves their pain points, we add far more value than our competitors. These clients will tell their friends about us, and our client list will grow. When your clients win, you win.

Without your clients, you have no business. At the start, it is easy to become focused on building your client list as quickly as possible. I believe your business will grow quicker if you focus on turning your client into a raving fan from the very first touchpoint. Your clients will be excited to do business with you and will refer people to you; even before you have sold them a deal. Keeping your investors is just as important as finding new investors.

Go and Do It

Our sales process follows a number of clear steps at KO Estates. This helps us to avoid any mistakes and protect our profit.

1. Present the Deal – The first step is presenting the deal. We spend a lot of time putting together an information pack so investors can see the value of the deal. This helps investors see if the deal is suitable for their needs, and we only receive calls from interested investors.
2. Proof of Funds – The next step is to confirm that the investor has the money to make the deal. This reduces the likelihood of the deal falling through. We check that the investor has the money in their account (either the deposit or the full amount depending on if they are paying cash or getting a mortgage). If they are getting a mortgage, then we also ask the buyer to provide a decision in principle to prove how much they will get from a mortgage.
3. Reservation Form – We sign a contract with the buyer to lock them into the deal. This protects the buyer, seller, and us because we're all bound by the contract. If the property needs work, the contract states that the buyer is on the hook for the cost of renovations.
4. Sourcing Fee – The buyer then pays a sourcing fee to secure the deal. This is non-refundable, so the vendor and I are compensated for our time if the deal falls through.
5. Memorandum of Sale – The final step is the Memorandum of Sale. This is a document that confirms the details of the sale.

Now the sale moves into the processing phase. It is largely in the hands of solicitors, but there is still a little bit of work to be done. We'll talk about that in the next chapter.

Progression

If I had written this book a year ago, I probably would have missed this chapter. Now, I can safely say that this is one of the most important chapters if you want to get paid for property sourcing. Closing the deal is only 50% of the work; the other 50% is progression.

My favourite motto is "the deal is not done until the deal is done." Ask the KO Estates team; I drill this into them. It is exciting when a client agrees to the sale, and we receive the sourcing fee and reservation fee. I don't want to kill that excitement, but we're only halfway there. We see clients through to completion.

Statistics show that 34% of sale agreements don't make it to completion. Can you believe that? After all that hard work, there is only a 66% chance that you will get paid. Well, I don't want to get paid on only 66% of the deals I sell. So, I had to create a strategy to beat the odds and increase my success.

When I first started property sourcing, I thought my job was about finding deals and selling them to investors. I thought it was job done once the deal was sold. But I soon discovered that wasn't the case at all.

Nobody talks about progression.

During the first year of my business, I worked hard to find deals, find investors, and get the sale agreed. I started to build up momentum, and over the course of 8 months, I sold 90 properties.

When I got the sale agreement and 50% sourcing fee, I celebrated. I thought the hard part was over. As far as I was concerned, the sale was in the hands of the solicitors to finish.

I was so wrong.

One day, I was speaking to an owner of an estate agency, and they were amazed at what I was doing. He asked me how I was managing the progressions. This conversation opened my eyes. He said that progression was one of the largest parts of the job. His estate agency employed several people full-time to handle the progressions. He asked me how I was managing the progressions of so many deals with such a lean team.

The short answer is we were not handling progressions at all.

Remember, I thought it was the job of the solicitors. At this point, I remember thinking I hadn't heard much at all from some of the early deals I sold. I checked on them, and they had dragged on for months. Some of the mortgage buyers were nearing the date of their mortgage offer expiry, big problem! Sometimes buyers can find a similar mortgage offer when that happens, and it only results in a small delay. Sometimes, they can't secure a mortgage, and the deal will fall through.

We were on the verge of losing money that I thought was guaranteed. It was a very stressful period because it also happened to fall during a period when the stamp duty holiday window was closing. Every property in the UK was desperately trying to meet the deadline because missing it would cost them thousands more.

With a large number of deals on the line, I was emailing and calling solicitors daily so we could turn it around and quick!

This was yet another lesson I learned the hard way. I had really neglected this part of the process, and it came back to bite me. In this short space of time, I learned what progression should look like. Turns out solicitors usually wait to be told what to do. They have hundreds of clients, so there is always another case to work on. In order to get the solicitors constantly working on the sale and moving things forward, all parties need to be in constant communication.

I definitely don't recommend trying to push through the months-long process within a week with the looming threat of a mortgage offer expiring. I needed these deals to go through; otherwise, I would be back to square one on multiple deals at the same time. My top tip to you is to get the deadline dates WAY ahead of time. I like to get the mortgage expiry date the day the client gets their offer. Get these dates in your calendar so you can see when they are coming up. No mad rush. Less stress for you and a better experience for your client.

The key to my progression strategy is what I like to call the 3 Cs of progression – communication, consistency, and clarity.

Communication

Your main role in the progression process is to facilitate communication between all parties. There are 4 people you need to keep track of:

- The vendor
- The vendor's solicitor

- The purchaser
- The purchaser's solicitor

You would think they are all working towards the same goal – completion. But they are not always singing from the same hymn sheet. Communication breakdowns result in delays. I cannot count the number of times progression has stopped because the purchaser thought they were waiting on information from the vendor, and the vendor thought they were waiting on information from the purchaser.

Checking in with everyone regularly helps to let everyone know what is going on and that no one is left in the dark. Use phone calls to clear up any confusion and then follow up with an email to summarise the conversation and serve as a reminder. The emails come in handy as a trail if you need to conduct an audit.

When communication stops, that's when you worry. When communication stops, it usually means progression has stopped too.

Consistency

Consistency is key to keeping progression moving along at a steady pace. You need to ensure that both sides are consistently making progress. Make contact with a party if they have an outstanding task to remind them that progress is halted until the task is complete.

I have never met a solicitor who isn't crazy busy. We're all busy, but solicitors are next-level busy. The old saying the squeaky wheel gets the grease applies here. Sometimes you need to follow up to get them to turn their attention back to the sale.

I make contact with solicitors weekly at a minimum, but some progressions need daily communication so that everyone understands exactly where we are and what we are waiting on. These updates help to push the process closer to completion. Pick the frequency that works for you, just know that consistent communication is what's needed to get the job done. You can't just chase once and move on to the next step.

Clarity

Our job is to make the process smooth and easy for everyone involved. In order to do that, we need to keep our communication simple and clear. Don't overcomplicate things. Understand what needs to be done and communicate it in the clearest manner possible.

Something you may have noticed from this chapter is that a lot of work goes into progression. If you are a one-person team like I was, you could handle progression for 1 or 2 deals per month. Once you start closing more than that, it is not manageable for one person – especially not if you want to keep finding and closing deals.

I closed over 90 deals in an 8-month period, so it was not remotely manageable for me to handle progression for that many deals alone, but I was not ready to hire an employee to handle it for me. Luckily, I came across a company that has become a major asset to my team. I outsource the progression process to them, and they handle all the communication on our behalf. When they call solicitors, vendors, and clients, they will introduce themselves by saying they are from KO Estates. This makes it seem like they are a full member of our team rather than us outsourcing the progression.

They only get paid if the sale completes, so it is in their interest to get the sale over the line too. Progression is their full-time job, so they are very experienced at what they do and have all day to spend on progression.

I catch up with the progression team once a week to discuss the sales, and they update me more regularly if necessary. It is a great way to get support with the progression process without having to hire and train full-time staff. It also saves me money on wages. As KO Estates grows, we may find it beneficial to have someone in-house, but for now, this works well.

Progression is a really important step of the sale, and it is easy to overlook when you first start your property sourcing business. The deal is not done until the deal is done. Take it from me; overlooking this step will do serious harm to your new business.

Go and Do It

The progression phase of the sale is an easy one to neglect for new property sourcers. It is one I neglected, and it almost came back to bite me. Even though the sale is now in the hands of solicitors, without the help of a third party, the sale often stalls. Both parties can easily become confused by what they are waiting for, and that confusion causes delays.

Progression is extremely time-consuming because it requires weekly or daily calls to keep the process moving along. I recommend outsourcing this when you're ready to a company that specialises in progression like I have. It is a lot more cost-effective than hiring someone to handle progression and having to train them.

Starting Your Property Sourcing Business

Setting up your business correctly from the start will make everything much easier. This chapter may seem boring, but legally it is one of the most important in the book. It will save you from stress and fines later on.

The sourcing industry is largely unregulated. In the past, it has given the property sourcing industry a bad name. But the good news is that the barrier to entry is low for property sourcing, and you can set up your business for a couple of hundred pounds. Here are the things you need.

Compliance

There are a few necessities you need to make sure your business is legal. Put these in place before you start operating.

HMRC Registration

Register your limited company with the HMRC to become incorporated. This saves your business name and makes your company official. I loved this part the most because it felt like my business was real, not just a hobby.

I incorporated my business 6 months before it officially began because I found a name I loved and wanted to make sure I claimed it. The KO of KO Estates is obviously my initials (Katie Orr), but it was also my nickname at school and at netball. I've always thought the KO was pretty cool and could be used as a play in words for a business name (though I thought it would be for a bar or something). While I have already used it for KO Estates, I have quite a few business ideas playing on my mind that the KO name would suit perfectly, so you might see some expansion in the future. It's a good job my parents picked the name Katie. At one point, they were thinking of naming me Amy, and I don't think AO would have worked so well.

Don't overthink your name; it doesn't have to be a perfect play on words or something really interesting and trendy. Just find something that you like and is memorable. For social media and website purposes, something concise works best.

It is not difficult to register your business as a limited company (LTD), but you can pay an accountant or solicitor to do it on your behalf. They will send you some paperwork to fill out, answer your questions, and file the paperwork correctly for you. It is only £12.50 to register your business yourself, but a solicitor or accountant will also charge you for your time. You can bundle this cost with other services like registering your business under their address.

When you register your business, it will need to be registered to a physical address. If you have an office space, that is the most logical address to use. Otherwise, you will have to register it under your home address or pay a service to use their address. I recommend paying to use your solicitor or accountant's address rather than your home address, especially if you are using social media for your business. The address for your business is easily accessed on Company

House's website, so it can put your safety at risk if you register your business under your home address.

When I first started KO Estates, I used my personal address for my business and thought nothing of it. When my videos started going viral, there was one troll who constantly put my home address in the comments alongside threatening messages. I quickly realised that it was a safety risk to have the home address for myself and my family so public. So, I paid to register my business under a different address. It only costs £20 per year, so it costs next to nothing.

Business Bank Account

You need a bank account for your business to keep things separate from your personal accounts. This makes life much easier when it comes to taxes and looks much more official to clients.

My recommendation is to start with an online bank like Monzo or Starling. They can get you set up in next to no time, and you can apply from home. You'll receive your business bank card in the mail within a week or two.

Property Ombudsman

There are two regulatory bodies that oversee property sourcing. These regulatory bodies exist to help in the case of disputes. Your clients can escalate complaints to your regulatory body, and you can seek dispute resolution services. You can choose between the two regulatory bodies, TPO (The Property Ombudsman) and PRS (Property Redress Scheme).

You are required by law to be a member of one of these schemes. If you're not, you could face fines of £5,000.

Both regulatory bodies offer similar services. The main differences are:

- Price –PRS offers lower-priced packages than TPO. This is great for property sourcers who are just starting their business.
- Rulings – TPO rulings are final and binding. The matter is settled, and you do not have to worry about the issue once the judgement has been made.
- The PRS is much lower cost and offers two pricing models for property sourcers. Research the packages and pick the best one for your needs. To apply to these regulatory bodies, you will need:
- Professional Indemnity Insurance (covered in the last point)
- Identification

Prices can vary, but they generally start at £135 per year.

Professional Indemnity Insurance

Professional Indemnity Insurance (PI insurance) is required for membership to the TPO or PRS.

This type of insurance covers your business if one of your clients claims that the property deal you sold was not as described. Instead of you having to pay thousands in damages and legal fees, your insurance company will investigate the claim and pay damages.

I recommend making sure your excess is low. I believe TPO requires it to be less than £1,000, but make sure it is an amount that you can easily pay if you lose a claim.

Prices can vary for PI insurance. Mine was £33 per month for the first year in business which added up to around £400 for the year.

Data Protection Fee

As property sourcers, we have access to confidential information for our investor lists and client information, so we need to be GDPR compliant. The Information Commissioners' Office charges a data protection fee to businesses that hold personal data. This fee is usually between £40-60 per year but varies depending on the business size in terms of staff and turnover.

I recommend taking the time to learn how to secure client data for your business. As your business grows, make sure your team can't access data they don't need to access.

Anti-Money Laundering

This is compulsory for all businesses connected to property sales, even solicitors. You need to register for anti-money laundering supervision with the HRMC and pay the fee, which is renewed annually. Property sourcing businesses register for this as if they were estate agents. This costs £300 per year.

£500 Property Sourcing Business

Starting a business doesn't have to cost an arm and a leg anymore. You can start a business for around £500. If it helps, think of that £500 as an investment in yourself. As a property sourcer, you can earn £5,000 in just one deal, so the return on your investment is HUGE.

- HMRC Registration £12.50
- Registered Address £20
- Anti-Money Laundering £300
- Redress Schemes £135
- Professional Indemnity Insurance £33

Total = £500.50

Please note that the costs discussed are accurate at the date of publishing. These prices are subject to change, so please check the price before you start.

If you co-source, then you can reduce these costs even more. Only one party in the collaboration needs to be registered, so co-sourcing is a great way to try property sourcing out before you commit £500. Try before you buy!

Go and Do It

You can start your business for very little cost if you stick to the essentials like the compliance section and your website and email address. Everything else just makes your life a little easier, but they can wait until you are profitable if you are on a budget.

Complete the following checklist to set up your business.

- Choose a business name
- Incorporate your business and register it with the HMRC
- Open a business bank account
- Create a simple website for your business
- Get a professional email address from your domain provider
- Purchase Professional Indemnity Insurance (PI insurance)

- Join a regulatory body like TPO or PRS
- Register for HMRC's anti-money laundering supervision
- Pay the ICO's Data Protection fee to be GDPR compliant

Scaling Your Property Sourcing Business

I became obsessed with selling deals. Once I had closed a sale, my mind would be on to the next one. It was never enough; I wanted to continue to grow KO Estates to bigger and better things.

This wasn't a 9-5 job; we would be closing deals at all times of the day. I remember being out celebrating a friend's birthday and I got a call from a client at 11.30 pm. I was many, many cocktails down at this point, but we had been working hard on this deal. I had to sober up in seconds, but I took the call and confirmed the sale of 4 properties. My friends were right there to celebrate the deal with me.

Being there for the customer when they needed us is what made our business unique. We worked around the client's schedule to make deals happen. This was something that Highstreet agents don't do, but we live in an age of convenience, and people expect this level of service. I expect this level of service, so that is why I like to be there for my clients.

Scale Profit

As much as I love property, I am in the property sourcing game to make money. So, the next step was to figure out how to make more money. The way I see it, there are two ways to increase your money when it comes to property sourcing:

1. Increase the number of deals
2. Increase the profit in each deal

Increase the Number of Deals

A great way to increase the rewards of an activity is to do more of it. It stands to reason that this is a great place to start if you want to scale your profits. When you first start your property sourcing business, your focus is to source and sell 1 deal. If you're anything like me, once you've sold your first deal, you want to scale this and quickly. I looked into the options; the obvious option was to continue what I was doing. So, I went out and found my next deal and sold it to my clients. The only thing was, I wanted to sell 100 properties in a year. That's a lot of vendors to meet and onboard. It's also a lot of buyers to work with.

To me, that seemed like a logistical nightmare. How would I ever have the time to speak to 200 people?! The admin alone! So instead, I started to look for vendors who had a portfolio they wanted to sell rather than individual houses. That would reduce the number of vendors I had to speak to and make 100 deals more doable. In my first year, most of my sales were from 2 vendors, 1 had a portfolio of 60 properties, and 1 had a portfolio of 40 properties. It was much more manageable working with just 2 vendors rather than 100. Think outside the box when you're scaling your property business. Work smarter, not harder.

Sourcing fees are typically 2-5% of the property price. The more properties you sell, the more you will earn. Selling more deals also means you will speak to more investors and expand your network.

When I was scaling my business, I charged a £2,000 sourcing fee for Buy to Let properties under 100k. Thinking back, it was probably undervalued, and that's why I had to scale my quantity to reach a 6-

figure year. At that time, I was still working full-time, and my property sourcing business took up all my nights and weekends. To say the time I had for my property sourcing business was limited is an understatement. I was working around the clock, missing out on events and social occasions to get everything done.

I was getting up at 5 am to go to the gym, working 8 am to 4 pm at my corporate job and then working on my property sourcing business until 11 pm at night. I was working myself to exhaustion. It left me making mistakes I would never usually make, and it had a negative effect on my health. I started getting rashes all over my skin due to the stress. I was burnt out and knew that what I was doing was not good for me or my body. If I had kept pushing myself, my mind or body would have broken down before long. I knew I couldn't continue, so I said enough was enough.

I quit my full-time job exactly a year to the day after I incorporated KO Estates. I was stretching myself too thin and knew it was time, but I was hesitant to leave behind the security of my 9-5. This felt like the biggest step so far in creating my business. In the end, I took it as a sign that it was the right time and seeing the date was the kick in the backside, I needed to bite the bullet and retire from my 9-5. Call it fate, call it looking for a reason to go all in, call it whatever you want. I needed some external reassurance that quitting my job was a good idea, and the date provided exactly that.

Getting Help

There are only a certain number of hours in a day, and property sourcing takes time. It takes time to find deals; it takes time to speak to clients. The model isn't scalable as a one-person operation because, at some point, you run out of hours. You can earn great money as a one-person operation and have multiple 6 figure years, but once you reach your time threshold, the only way to scale further is to add more people to your team.

When I reached that point, I knew something needed to change. I couldn't possibly do everything myself, and if I was going to scale, I needed some support.

I wrote down everything that I felt I could hand off. The obvious starting place was the task that was taking up most of my time – customer communication. To be more specific, communicating with clients on social media platforms. We were getting hundreds of messages a day from clients on social media, and I was having a hard time keeping up with them. These messages were from people wanting help, and all of them had the potential to result in a sale. I couldn't ignore them.

I advise handing off some tasks as soon as possible and as soon as your business can afford it to escape burnout. Start by getting rid of the tasks you hate most or the tasks that consume the most time. You don't have to do it all yourself.

As a side note, it gets worse before it gets better. I don't want to be a Negative Nelly, but I do want to keep it real. I thought that hiring help was going to be an overnight fix. I thought that as soon as they started, I would feel relaxed. Unfortunately, it is not that quick or easy. If it were that easy, everyone would be doing it. I thought that I would hire someone, and they would have a massive impact the very next day.

There is a large upfront time commitment to train someone to do what you do. You can't expect someone to pick up your work without any help or support. This training is important to help them do the tasks to your standards, but it does require you to invest time in training them. Not ideal if your schedule is already packed, but this upfront work is crucial to success further down the line. The more training you give them, the better job they will be able to do in the future.

Training someone to take some tasks off your plate will allow you to increase the number of deals you provide. Increasing the number of deals you do is a healthy way to grow the business. You learn a lot with each deal and establish yourself as an expert. Doing more deals will help you to build trust.

Just remember that property sourcing is not passive, and there is a ceiling to your time. Be mindful of how long each deal will take you, and try to anticipate when you need to bring on help before you reach that ceiling. Outsource tasks or hire a team member in order to free up your time to concentrate on more important parts of your business.

There are many ways you can do this aside from hiring a full-time member of staff. You could hire a part-timer to provide a few extra hours a week. You could hire a freelancer or subcontractor to provide expertise. This is often for a short-term project, but it could be to complete a small task on a regular basis. You could even outsource a task to another business like I did with progression. I would recommend starting with a virtual assistant. You can pay them to help you out with a number of admin tasks for a few hours per week. Some virtual assistants even have special skills like video editing or content writing, so they can provide support with recurring business tasks. Starting with freelancers and subcontractors can minimise the risk when you first begin scaling your business.

For me, the very first thing I needed to take off my plate was managing my Instagram messages. I was staying up late at night to answer these messages, and I was so tired it felt like my eyes were bleeding. After a breakdown and a few tears, I knew I needed to hire some help. So, I decided to hire someone to help for a few hours each day just to answer my Instagram messages. It took a little bit of time to give them the initial training, and then I was able to take a backseat. My first hire was my best friend Katie (how great are friends!) who worked on an hourly basis to help me deal with my Instagram messages. By that point, a few of my posts were going viral, and my Instagram messages were blowing up with people wanting more information. It was time-consuming to answer all of these, and it took me away from finding deals and selling them to clients. I knew that getting back to people was important, but finding and selling deals were the best uses of my time. So, I needed to hire so I could develop my pipeline of customers

I paid Kate hourly, and it was completely risk-free because I could scale up and down as needed. It meant I didn't have to commit to paying an entire salary before I knew for sure that I could support someone. I got back my time and happiness, so it was a no-brainer!

Since then, the fabulous KO Estates team has grown to 8, and we have huge plans for growth. KO Estates wouldn't be where it is today without the hard work and expertise of our team. When it comes to hiring, hire people who are better than you and share your goals, and you will become an unstoppable force. I learn so much from my team on a daily basis, and the things they do blow me away. I wouldn't have it any other way!

Increase the Profit in Each Deal

I could continue to scale the team and number of deals, but I was stretched to my limits, and I was completely new to managing people, so I wanted to get it right before I scaled aggressively. The other obvious option to increase my profits was increasing the sourcing fee I charged for each deal. But I work for the client when I source property deals, so it would be unethical of me to add an unreasonable sourcing fee. It would affect their numbers and their ROI (return on investment). At the end of the day, it was not something I was willing to do. If I could increase the value I was offering my clients, then I could justify increasing my sourcing fee. If I helped them to achieve more, I could justify charging more.

My network had been growing, and people were starting to learn more about what I was doing. One day, I received a phone call from a landlord who was looking to sell his portfolio of properties. He wanted to scale down and pull some cash out.

This was brilliant news for me; I had secured more stock.

The one condition was the vendor wanted a quick and easy sale. Normally, in this situation, I would've broken the portfolio down and sold the properties individually. When we sell that many properties individually at a fast rate, it is anything but easy for the vendor. The last vendor I worked with said that they had never been busier in their life. They got the fast sales they were looking for, but they also had to go through the sales process of 60 properties. I learned from that feedback, and so when this vendor told me they wanted an easy sale, I knew that we had to sell the portfolio as a whole rather than individually. This gave me an opportunity to add value on both sides by making things easier for both the vendor and my client.

Luckily for me, this was around the time I met my boyfriend, Jake, who had been involved in real estate for 6 years. He has tonnes of experience with large transactions because he has been working with overseas investors (which means cash buyers). My clients were mainly UK clients, so he brought a lot of knowledge and a different approach to the table. He partnered with me on this sale and taught me a lot about selling multi-million-pound deals.

This sale marked a turning point in my business. I had never worked on a deal at this scale before; up until this point, I had sold a maximum of 5 properties in a single deal. It opened my eyes to what was possible for KO Estates. The deal took the same amount of time as the single property deals I sold, but the sourcing fee was significantly more.

I brought the property portfolio to the table, and Jake brought a high-net-worth client; it was a win-win. But more than that, I learned how to structure a deal like this, and now I can repeat it to grow my business. This is the biggest benefit of partnering with others in the industry. You can learn from someone else in the business, and sometimes, this opens your eyes to opportunities that you didn't know existed. Learn from as many people as you can. Everyone has a different way of doing things, and you never know what ideas may come from your collaborations.

It was a clean portfolio sale, and both the buyer and vendor were extremely happy. Due to the size of the portfolio, I was able to secure a £115,000 sourcing fee on the transaction. I worked to understand what was important to both parties and packaged the deal in a way that both the vendor and purchaser were happy. A fast, easy process was important to both the vendor and buyers, so I added a huge amount of value there. Increasing the value allowed me to nearly 3 times more than I otherwise would have. This was when I knew I could scale my sourcing business much further without the need for a huge team. I much prefer a lean team.

Portfolios are harder to come by, and this portfolio was an absolute dream. Each property had tenants in place and great cash flow. It was a perfect opportunity for an investor who had a considerable amount of money to invest. It offered a much more hands-off approach than building a portfolio from scratch. There would be fewer problems, fewer costs, and there was a proven track record for each property.

Don't be scared to take on bigger deals; they take just as much time to close as a small deal, but you get paid more. This is how your business becomes scalable because you are charging more for the same amount of time. There is more due diligence involved, but aside from that, a multi-million-dollar deal is much the same as a £100,000 deal.

Higher fees come with larger deals. Property sourcing fees are often charged as a percentage, usually between 2-5%. Larger deals mean more work which means you can charge a higher percentage.

There are more hoops to jump through with larger portfolios or certain property types, like commercial properties. You have more legal considerations, so you need to get paid more for that because your expertise comes into play.

Basically, you are getting paid more because the deal is more complex, and both parties need your expertise. You do a lot more work in negotiating, packaging the deal, and qualifying the investor.

Don't be afraid to charge a higher fee for more complex deals; investors understand that they get what they pay for. If you are saving your client a lot of money, for example, your deal is 20% off the market value, then they don't mind paying you a higher sourcing fee. You can push a 5-6% sourcing fee because the value you gave them far outweighs your fee. It's still a win-win for everyone. Don't underestimate the value you provide. Your deal could give a client passive income for life or a £20,000 profit on a flip. Be confident in your worth and your sourcing fee.

Like with anything else, the more value you add, the more you will get paid. If you continually provide more value than your competition, you will never go out of business.

Investors learn to diversify their portfolios, and I think that lesson can be applied to business. Chase the big deals if you want, but don't pass over easy wins. Sometimes it takes a little bit of time to build enough trust to land the big deals, so the small deals will keep the lights on in the meantime. My low-price Buy to Let deals produce most of the cash flow for my business; the bigger deals are a very welcomed bonus. Both are important for scaling your business.

Other Ways to Maximise Income

If we boil it down to the simplest terms, maximising your business's income comes down to two things:

1. Reducing the cost of a deal (closing deals faster and cheaper, so you have more resources to take on extra deals)
2. Increasing the income in a deal (add on extra products and services so that your sourcing fee is not the only way to make money)

Look at every single element of your business and see if there is a way you can optimise it. Is there a way you can reduce costs or increase the return on investment for any of your resources? Here are some ideas to get you started.

Partner With Other Businesses

This is an easy win for you and your clients. Your clients receive a list of trusted local property services to get them from A to close. They need solicitors, mortgage advisors, surveyors, and letting agents. If they are first-time buyers or not local to the area, they will appreciate getting a list of recommendations to save them time researching.

You win because you can ask for a referral fee from these businesses, maximising the profit in each deal. Also, when your clients work with a team of experts, it makes the process go smoothly. If even one of the people involved drops the ball, the sale could fall through, so it's in your best interest to have your clients working with the best in the business. Your client's team can literally make or break the sale.

I like to call the people I recommend the dream team. I have hand-selected them from my own experiences buying my properties, and I know they will provide high-quality services to my clients. Reach out to people you want to recommend and see if they would partner with you. Many of these businesses have referral schemes in place already, but you can ask for a referral or affiliate fee for each client you introduce. You could pick up an extra £1,000 on each deal if the client works with everyone you recommend. This adds up quickly and increases your profit for very little work. Make sure you have a signed agreement with them so everyone knows what they are getting into and is protected.

Automate Repetitive Tasks

It doesn't matter if you are looking to grow your business enough to leave your corporate job or if you want to scale property sourcing to a 7-figure business. You will reach a point where you cannot scale any further because you have run out of hours in a day. Property sourcing takes time.

Luckily for me, my corporate job was big on refining processes and looking for more efficient ways to do things. This is something I implement in my business every day. I ask myself, *how can we do this better? How can we save time?* At the end of the day, time is money. When I was a one-woman operation, I wanted to take as many tasks off my plate as possible, so I could focus on selling more deals. Even now, I have a small team. I want to reclaim as much time as possible for my team to reduce the number of people I need to hire. Using Calendly instead of my phone ringing off the hook or hiring someone to answer my phone was a great example of this. Another thing I implemented early on was creating templates for presenting deals or other common emails so I could modify them instead of typing them all from scratch.

There are a lot of things you can automate in order to save time. I recommend looking for things you can automate before you start hiring a team. My strategy has always been to stay as lean as possible and only hire for tasks that I cannot automate. Hiring staff is a huge expense, and it adds a lot of pressure. There will come a time when hiring a team is necessary to continue to scale, but until then, automate!

<u>Subscription Model</u>

Another great way to increase your profits is to offer a subscription model. This works best when you are more established and have a sizeable investor list full of clients hungry for deals.

A subscription model creates a steady income stream that provides your business with a little bit of security. You can count on the income from your subscriptions each month. It can be a lifesaver when you are looking to expand your team.

There are so many different types of subscriptions you could offer, depending on the type of clients you serve. Your subscription model should be a member club where clients pay a monthly fee to receive membership and associated benefits. As a property sourcer, one of the best benefits you can provide is early access to deals.

You want the club to feel exclusive and special in order to get people excited to join. It helps to build a sense of community within the membership club. Your clients will appreciate the opportunity to surround themselves with like-minded people. It gives them a sense of belonging and helps them feel more connected. Both are essential ingredients to create a base of loyal, raving fans.

I created KO-MMUNITY (a bit of a play on words), where members get:

- Access to an online community
- Early access to deals
- Property education and training
- Monthly calls
- Property news and updates

I love it because I get to connect on a regular basis with my most loyal customers. It offers an easy way to reward my raving fans and give back to them. I can also understand their pain points better and figure out how to alleviate their problems so they can achieve their goals. Through KO-MMUNITY I can get to know them on a much more personal level. It's a great way to listen to the market.

When you start a subscription model, it requires consistent work. I review KO-MMUNITY and make improvements constantly. I try and pop in to chat and add new resources as often as I can. Don't start a subscription model as a way to make easy money. It brings consistent money, but it does need consistent work. Your subscribers or club members are paying for more access to you and more value, so you need to make sure you provide that.

The sky is the limit when it comes to ways to produce more income for your business. One of the best places to start is to calculate the cost of each deal you sell and the total income in each deal you sell. Write down all the costs involved in selling a deal, including how much you spend on wages and outsourcing. Then list all sources of income in a deal, not only your sourcing fee but anything additional such as affiliate fees from partnerships.

Go and Do It

You have sold your first few deals. Now it is time to scale your business. There are two main ways to scale your property sourcing business:

1. Sell more deals
2. Increase the profit in your deals

A combination of the two is usually the best approach. The main thing to remember is that property sourcing takes time. There will come a point where you reach the ceiling on the number of deals you sell because you simply don't have more time to give. It is at that point that you need to outsource tasks or hire staff to give you more time to sell deals and look for ways to increase the profit in your deals.

Another option is to find additional income streams for your business. KO Estates has the following income streams on top of selling deals:

- Referral fees – we get a payment for referring clients to property professionals in the area. It is a win-win because the clients need mortgage advisor or solicitor recommendations, and we earn a little bit more on the deal.
- Subscription model – we have a clubhouse membership, KO-MMUNITY, where investors get early access to deals, property investing education, and a community of like-

minded individuals. This subscription service has given our business a consistent income stream.

Write down your ideas for additional income streams when you have them. Sometimes ideas don't work right now, but they could work for your business in the future.

Mindset

So far in this book, we have covered the technical skills needed to start a property business. Like anything else, these are skills that can be learned by anyone. The thing that stops most people who want to try property sourcing is not the deals. They get in their own way. It mainly comes down to a fear of failure and a fear of what other people will think. Many people fear what their friends or family will say or what people will think if it doesn't work out. Fear is stopping you from putting the work in to achieve your goal.

I got over my fear of failure when I asked myself what I was more afraid of, trying and failing or not trying at all. Either way, I could potentially fail, but trying would give me the best chance of success. When you put it like that, the logic is hard to argue against. Still, it takes a lot of logic to overcome your emotions.

Try weighing up the pros and cons of trying, even if it leads to failure. Here is the list I made when I did this.

Pro's	Cons
I could earn much more	It doesn't work out
I can be my own boss	
I have freedom	

I can work wherever I want	
I can work whenever I want	
I can follow my passion	
I can have more time to spend with family	
I can experience so much more	
I can treat my friends and family	
I can be generous with time and money	
It will work for me	

Chances are, your pro list will outweigh the cons, just like in my list. Do you want to give up the opportunity to experience all of those pros because you are worried it might not work out? Your business will work out. My business worked, and it will work for you too. Be certain of your success, and then work backwards to find the steps you need to take.

Thinking that your business won't work out is the worst position to be in. You have to be 100% certain that your business will be successful. If you are, then your brain will approach problems in a different way when they arise. When you know your business will be successful, your brain approaches problems knowing everything will work out. It looks for solutions rather than throwing in the towel.

Someone once said it's like a child learning to walk. The child doesn't give up and decide, "walking mustn't be for me" after falling over a few times. It keeps trying until it gets it. You need to approach your business in the same way.

If you focus on what will happen if you fail, you will not put your all into the business. You will not reach your full potential. I get it; no one wants to face embarrassment, fear, or shame. This fear stops a lot of people from achieving their dreams. Stop thinking about what will happen if you fail, and start thinking about what your life will look like if you succeed. I know which outcome I want more. Which one do you want?

Here are some other things that will determine your success.

Time

We all have the same 24 hours in a day. Not everyone is on equal playing field, and some people have more commitments than others, but you can find time if you look for it.

If you want to start a successful business, you need to make some sacrifices to put more time into your business. You may need to get up earlier or reduce the time you spend watching TV. I wake up at 5 am in order to get some deep work done before the rest of the world wakes up. After 9 am, my day is full of phone calls, meetings, and emails. I am constantly distracted and can't get any solid work done, so those few hours in the morning are key to growing my business. I love waking up at 5 am, but I use that time to write marketing emails or update my website. Currently, I am using this time to write my book.

When I first started KO Estates, I had a full-time job, and my schedule looked different. I would work out at 6 am, start my job at 8 am and work until 4 or 5 pm. My evenings were for KO Estates, and I would work until 11 pm at night most nights.

My schedule has changed over time, but the foundations are the same. I schedule out time for the most important tasks of the day. These are the non-negotiables, and everything else needs to work around them. I also identify which balls I can drop if I become overwhelmed or an emergency derails my day. Knowing these two things are key to managing my time. I love KO Estates and finding deals for clients, so most of the time, I can't wait to start work. I think a schedule is also useful to give you discipline on the days when you are tired or unmotivated. Scheduling helps to keep me focused when I need an extra push to get things done.

Set Goals

I get very excited about a new idea, but there is a rational, sensible, boring part of my brain that is worried about the risk. I wish I could turn off that part of my brain. It is the part of my brain that made me nervous about leaving my full-time job. It told me that my job gave me security and perks. I had a mortgage to pay.

I knew if I wanted to get to a place where I could work to live rather than live to work, I needed to scale my business enough to shut up the risk-averse part of my brain. I needed it quiet to give me the confidence to take the leap. If I were going to do this, I was going to be the best.

I started by identifying what my goal was. What would it look like if I achieved my goal? Then, I identified why I wanted to achieve that goal. I was looking back through my diary recently and found my goals page it said "to our earn my 9-5 and leave by April 2021"

Writing this goal down was a pivotal moment for me. I hadn't started my blog back in 2019. KO Estates was not even a thought. I just knew that the 9-5 life was not for me.

When I wrote that, I had no idea how I would achieve that goal or what the process would look like. I just focused on the end goal and thought about it every day. I daydreamed about handing in my notice and living life on my own terms.

Your goal doesn't have to be the same as mine. You may not want to leave your job; you may pursue property sourcing as a side hustle or to learn more. There is no right or wrong goal. You just need to have something to work towards so you can measure progress. Your goal could be a monthly profit goal, it could be a number of properties you want to sell, or even something you are saving for. Having a measurable goal will hold you accountable and ensure you are making progress towards it.

So much talk about goal setting gets hung up on the HOW. I agree that when you want to achieve something specific, you do need to really reverse engineer the process. That being said, it is also okay to have a big, scary, far-off goal and not know how you are going to get there yet. When you do that, I think you are more open to opportunities that come across your path rather than waiting around for something specific. There are many different ways to achieve your goals, so don't close yourself off to alternative paths.

Leaving my job was one of the biggest, scariest decisions I have made to date. I was excited to work full-time on my business and maybe get some of my leisure time back. That didn't mean I wasn't terrified to leave the security of having a full-time job and give up the company perks. Comfort can be really detrimental to success. As humans, we are reluctant to give up comfort, but that reluctance can stop us from moving on to bigger and better things. It is easy to see how people stay in a job for 30+ years. They are comfortable, and moving out of that comfort zone is painful.

How Do You Eat an Elephant?

Anything you want to achieve can be boiled down to a 5-minute task. I remind myself this when I feel overwhelmed and don't know where to start, and I ask myself, what is the next best step I can take? Nobody climbs Everest in a single step, the climb is broken down into smaller checkpoints and they concentrate on one step at a time. Instead of looking at an overwhelming task as a whole, just look for one action you can take right now to get moving in the right direction. It may be watching a video, scheduling a call, or joining a programme. When you break it into bite-sized pieces, it becomes more manageable.

It is really easy to get overwhelmed when starting a business. There is so much to do, and it seems like a monumental task. Break things down into more manageable pieces and focus on the next thing. As the saying goes, Rome wasn't built in a day. It was achieved one project or one task at a time.

Take one step today to move closer to your goal. Then do the same tomorrow. In a few months, when you look back, you will be surprised at how far you have come and the results you have achieved. Don't get bogged down in the minor details. Just start.

Believe In the Service You Provide

There are plenty of people out there looking to spend money on property. There is everything from first-time investors looking to create passive income to funds looking to spend millions. We need to make sure we are getting a piece of the action.

If you hate selling, it helps to frame it as serving rather than selling. People are looking for something to invest their money into. At the moment, keeping savings in a bank will provide 1% interest if you are lucky. It is not even keeping up with inflation, so people are looking for more effective ways to grow their money.

You are losing money by keeping it in the bank rather than investing it. Your interest rates will not keep up with inflation, so your savings become less valuable the longer they sit there. As a property sourcer, you're not just finding investment properties; you are preventing them from losing money. In my niche, I am showing investors that they don't need to be millionaires in order to invest in property.

We act almost like wealth managers by finding opportunities for clients to achieve a good return on their investment. So, we bring an attractive offer to the table.

Go and Do It

Your mindset is a key factor in your success. If you are scared of what other people think or scared of failure, then you will not put 100% into your business. Your negative mindset will hold you back.

There is always a chance a business might fail, but I would rather know that I put in maximum effort. For me, it would be frustrating to have a business fail because I just didn't try hard enough. I found success with property sourcing when I had no idea what I was doing. So, you will succeed. Believe it. This book gives you all the information you need to succeed, so you already have a better chance of success than I ever did.

- Believe in yourself and your business
- Prioritise your time on activities that will help you to succeed
- Dare to dream big

REPLICATE SUCCESS

In November 2021, I was at the Negotiator Awards. I had received an exciting letter in the post a few months prior telling me I had been nominated in 3 categories:

1. Rising Star of the Year
2. Marketing Campaign of the Year
3. New Agency of the Year

I looked it up and quickly realised that I had been nominated in 3 categories at the Oscars of the property world. Needless to say, I was excited. I bought a new dress and shoes and headed down to London, excited for the event. I didn't expect to win anything, but I was looking forward to a swanky night out.

The event was held at the decked-out Grosvenor Hotel. It was a black-tie event with big industry leaders among the 350 guests. I was a little overwhelmed, to be honest. We had been in business for 9 months and didn't even have enough people to fill a whole table. As I mingled and met new people, I kept the fact that I was a sole property sourcer and ran my business from my bedroom tightly under wraps. Everyone else was from huge national chains, so I felt super out of place. Imposter syndrome is something that I have struggled with my whole life, and it was back in full force this night. Imagine my surprise when I learned that I was the only person out of the 350 attendees to be nominated in 3 categories. It was the proudest moment of my life and one I will never forget.

I went in with zero expectations, but I came away highly commended in 2 categories: Rising Star of the Year and Marketing Campaign of the Year. Chuffed! My story is a testament to the fact that you can learn the technical skills as you go. I had no idea what I was doing when I started; I didn't even know what a property sourcer was. You are already way ahead of me.

The biggest hurdle is often yourself. Think of any other job you had or any other time you have tried something new. You learned the skills as you went by doing the damn thing and looking to people around you for guidance. If you want to accelerate the process of picking up skills, you seek out a mentor to provide you with information and answer the questions you have.

I am a big believer in replicating success. I think if there is someone out there doing what you want to do and achieving the results you want, they are the best person to learn from. Understand what they do, how they do it, and why they do it and replicate it. It's like following a recipe.

When you cook or bake, you are following an expert's blueprint. The chef or baker has spent years perfecting their recipe. When you follow their recipe, you can skip all those years of work to achieve the same result. It would make no sense to try baking for the first time and make up a recipe yourself. Why wouldn't you follow a recipe if there was one available? It saves you time and costly errors.

I stumbled through deal sourcing at the very beginning. I am not too proud to admit that I had no idea what I was doing. Deal sourcing literally fell into my lap after people asked questions following my first viral post.

This means that I figured a lot of things out for myself through trial and error. I made a whole lot of mistakes and spent a lot of time on Google. Seriously, my training consisted of learning by doing and looking things up on Google and YouTube.

If you want results in the quickest possible time, don't try and do everything yourself and learn everything the hard way. There are a lot of people out there who have gone before you, and you can learn from their experiences and mistakes. Replicating success is all about following a blueprint to build your business on a solid foundation. I would advise doing this as early as possible to speed up your success. It's like having a premier league coach on your team instead of just learning skills in your back garden.

In this book, I have broken down the fundamental elements of deal sourcing. You have just read 11 chapters that take you through how to get set up, how to find and sell deals, and how to scale your property sourcing business. Now it is up to you to put my advice into practice and start your property sourcing business.

You don't have to do it alone. If you need more support, join my Sourcing Success Programme to receive guidance along the way. It's A group of incredible people growing their business from strength to strength. I feel I have found my people through this programme!

Without sounding dramatic, property sourcing has changed my life. In my first 12 months of operations, I earned over £100,000. This was over 3 times what I was earning in my corporate 9-5, and I was doing something I loved. I mean, I'm making money by helping other people make money and achieve their goals. How cool is that?

Property sourcing allowed me to leave my full-time job and follow my passions all while working whenever and wherever I wanted. I was finally in charge of how much I earnt. It has been an amazing journey, and I wrote this book and created my Sourcing Success course to help other people find the freedom I have.

Thank you for buying this book, and congratulations on reading it until the end. I recently heard a statistic that blew me away. Only 60% of all books purchased are read. Even less get finished. So, I know you are here because you are serious about taking action. Run with that enthusiasm and use the momentum you have built to start your property sourcing business.

My final piece of advice to you is to just start. Go for it. Think of where you will be a year from now.

Thanks so much for your time; I hope you got some real value from everything we went through. I would love to hear from you know what you thought of the book. Make sure to share your learnings and tag me on socials, I would love to hear from you about your property journey. Let's do it together! If you would like any further information on the Sourcing Secrets programme, head to

www.property-sourcing-secrets.com/join-now

Instagram: @Katieorr___

KO Estates 1st Birthday

Celebrating with best friend

KO Estates HQ

Sometime my office is this

Working with Hong Kong Investors

On a new development site checking opportunities for clients

Finding Time for content daily

Printed in Great Britain
by Amazon